The following story is an excerpt from TOKYOPOP's next STAR TREK THE MANGA Anthology KAKAN NI SHINKOU, available in stores September 2007.

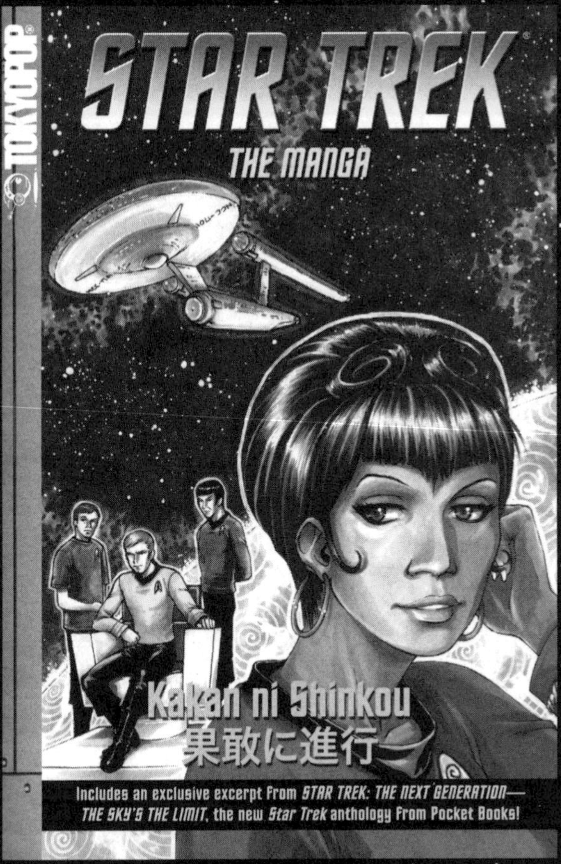
TOKYOPOP
STAR TREK
THE MANGA
Kakan ni Shinkou
果敢に進行
Includes an exclusive excerpt from STAR TREK: THE NEXT GENERATION—
THE SKY'S THE LIMIT, the new Star Trek anthology from Pocket Books!

Manga. The Final Frontier. These are the voyages of the starship Enterprise...

In KAKAN NI SHINKOU: Kirk is put on trial for crimes he has yet to discover... Uhura demonstrates the true power of communication... Bones gets to the core of Vulcan emotion... Scotty has to extract dilithium crystals from a mine in the middle of a war zone... and an alien delegation uses the Enterprise as a vessel of deception! Featuring:

CURA TE IPSUM
Story by Wil Wheaton
Art by EJ Su

SCAEAN GATE
Story by Diane Duane
Art by Don Hudson

COMMUNICATIONS BREAKDOWN
Story by Christine Boylan
Art by Bettina Kurkoski

THE TRIAL
Story by Mike Wellman
Art by Nam Kim

FORGING ALLIANCES
Story by Paul Benjamin
Art by Steven Cummings

Also check out TOKYOPOP's first STAR TREK THE MANGA Anthology SHINSEI/SHINSEI

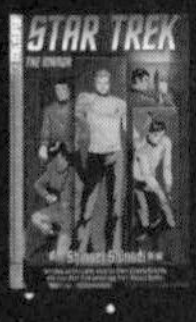
STAR TREK

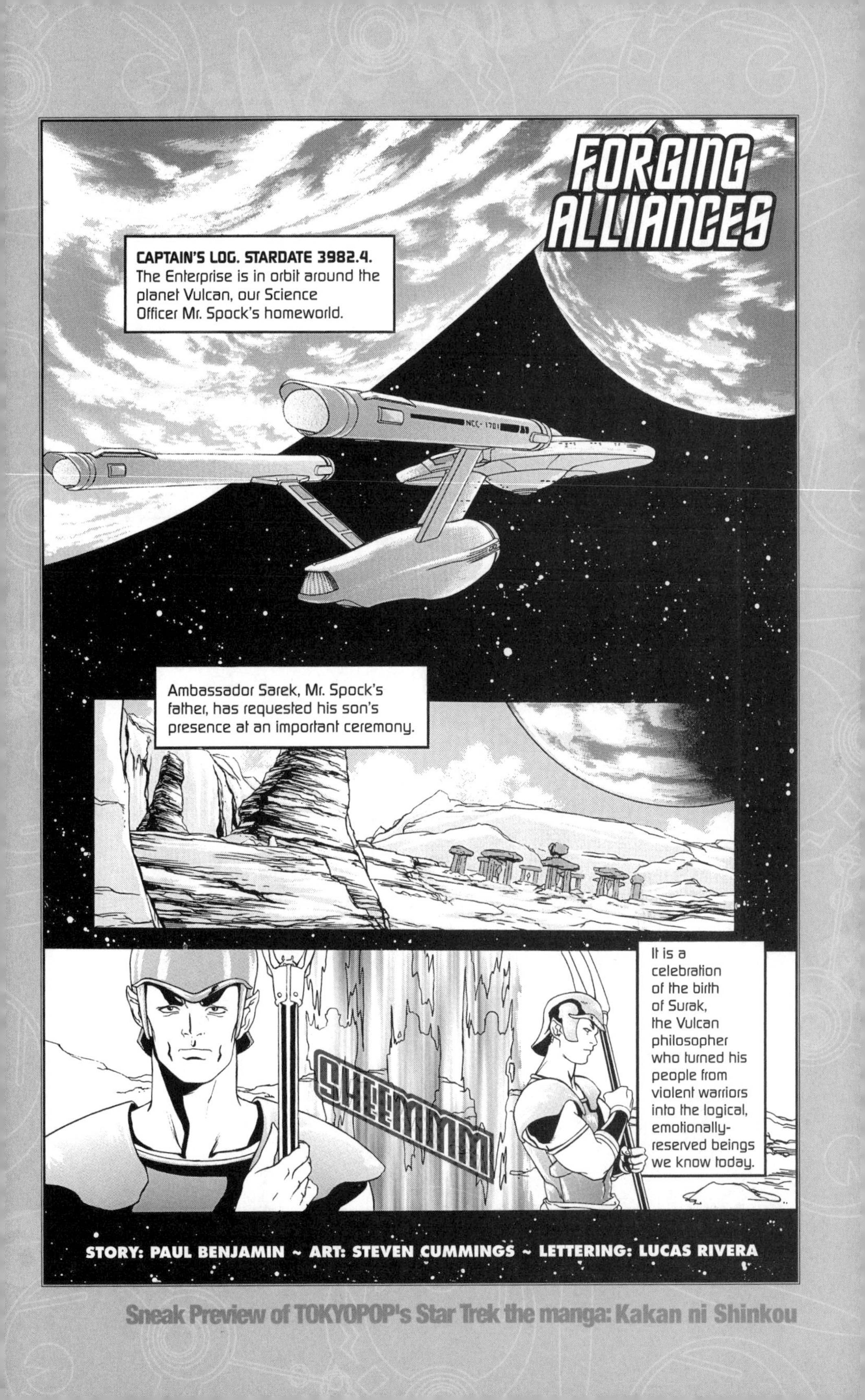
FORGING ALLIANCES
CAPTAIN'S LOG. STARDATE 3982.4. The Enterprise is in orbit around the planet Vulcan, our Science Officer Mr. Spock's homeworld.
NCC-1701
Ambassador Sarek, Mr. Spock's father, has requested his son's presence at an important ceremony.
SHEEMMM
It is a celebration of the birth of Surak, the Vulcan philosopher who turned his people from violent warriors into the logical, emotionally-reserved beings we know today.
STORY: PAUL BENJAMIN ~ ART: STEVEN CUMMINGS ~ LETTERING: LUCAS RIVERA

Sneak Preview of TOKYOPOP's Star Trek the manga: Kakan ni Shinkou

LIVE LONG AND PROSPER, FATHER.
PEACE AND LONG LIFE, MY SON.
CAPTAIN KIRK AND DR. MCCOY. THOUGH YOU ARE OUT-WORLDERS, YOU HAVE BEEN TRUE FRIENDS TO MY SON AND WILL BE ALLOWED TO OBSERVE THE T'VED-SURAK RITUAL.
THANK YOU, AMBASS-ADOR SAREK. WE WOULD BE HONORED.
CAREFUL, JIM. START TALKING LIKE THEM NOW AND BEFORE YOU KNOW IT OUR EARTH PARTIES WILL BE AS RIGID AS THESE VULCAN CEREMONIES.

Sneak Preview of TOKYOPOP's Star Trek the manga: Kakan ni Shinkou

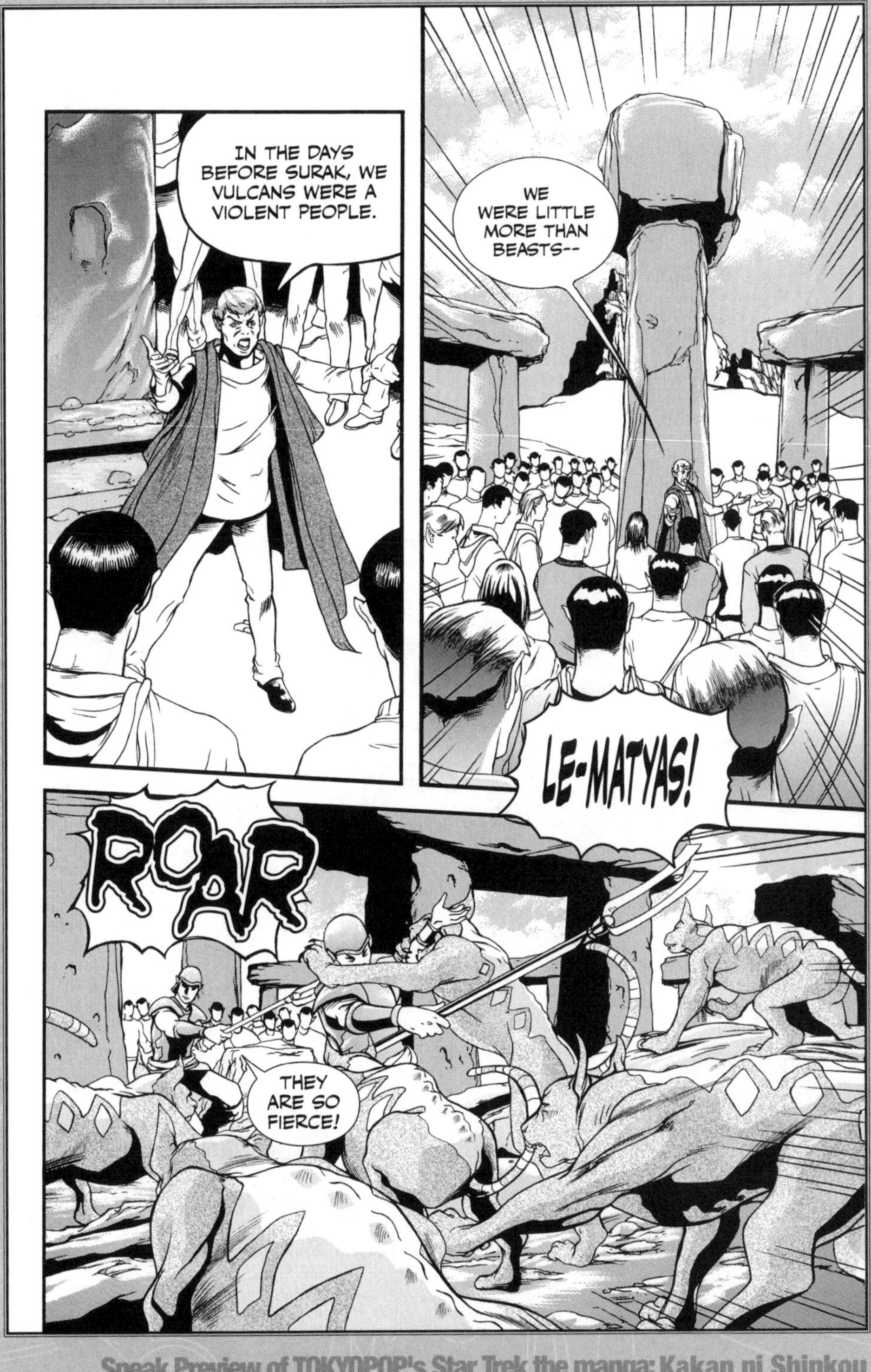
IN THE DAYS BEFORE SURAK, WE VULCANS WERE A VIOLENT PEOPLE.
WE WERE LITTLE MORE THAN BEASTS--
LE-MATYAS!
ROAR
THEY ARE SO FIERCE!

Sneak Preview of TOKYOPOP's Star Trek the manga: Kakan ni Shinkou

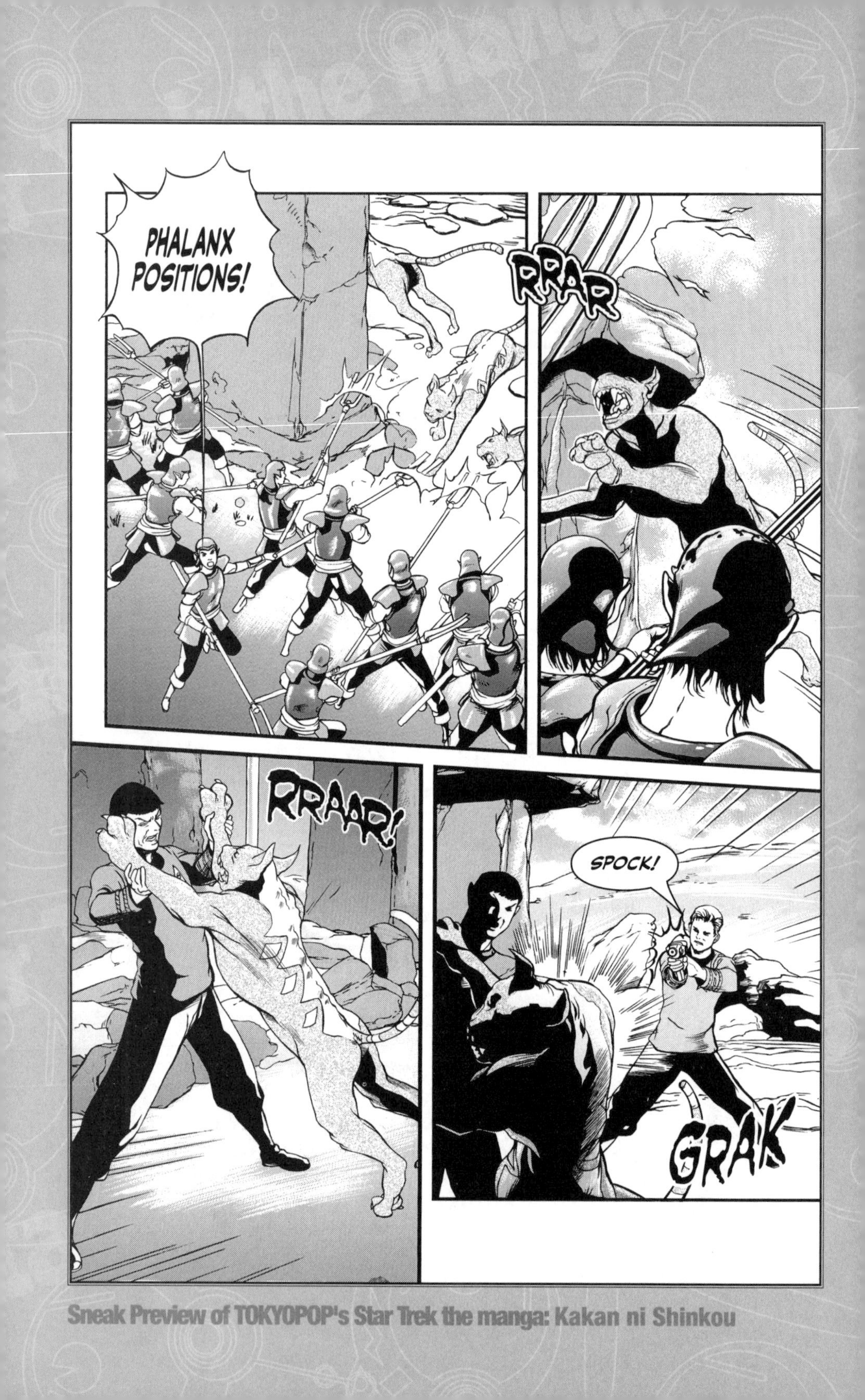
PHALANX POSITIONS!
RRAR
RRAAR!
SPOCK!
GRAK

Sneak Preview of TOKYOPOP's Star Trek the manga: Kakan ni Shinkou

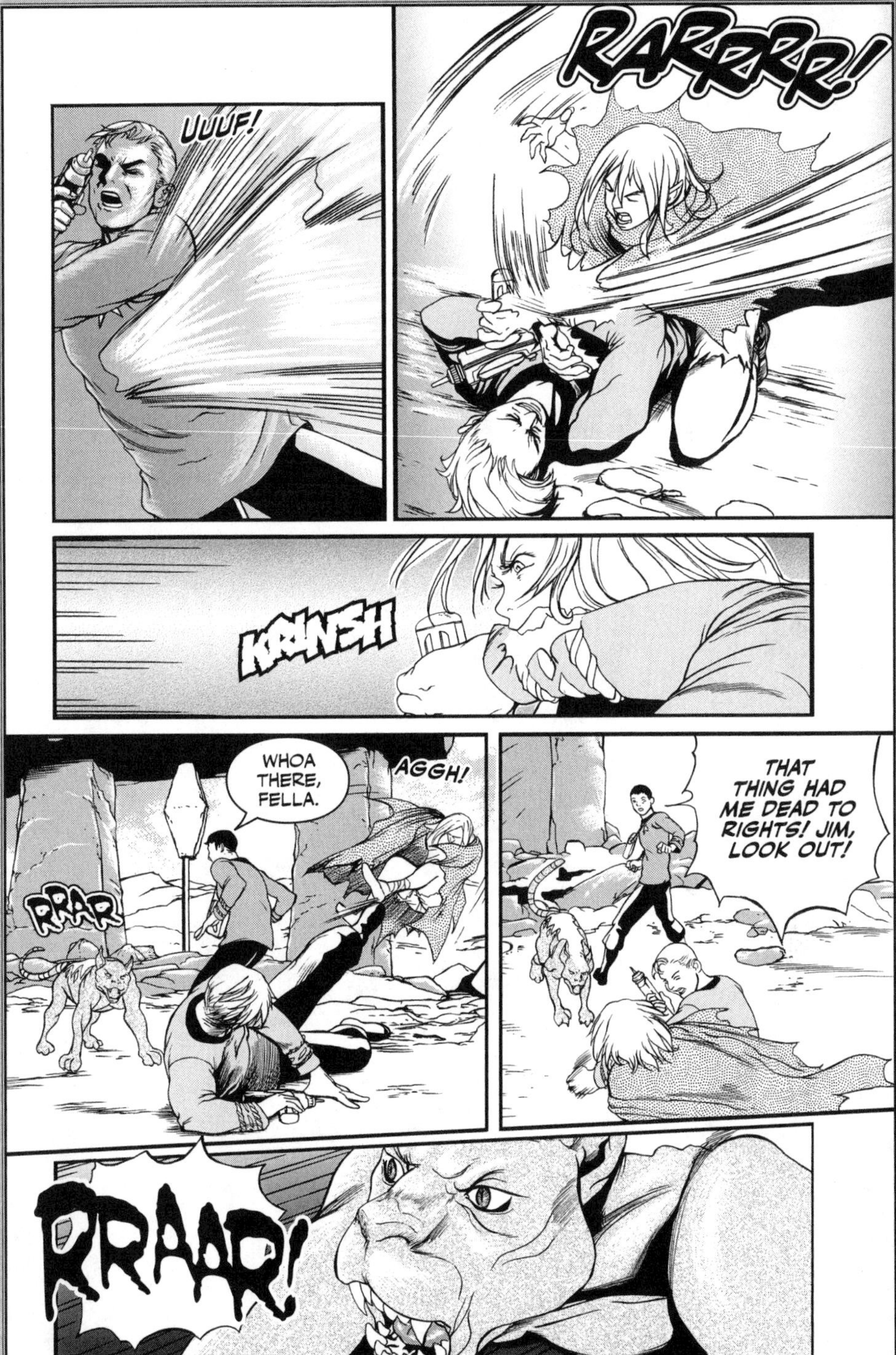
UUUF!
RARRRR!
KRUNSH
WHOA THERE, FELLA.
AGGH!
RRAR
THAT THING HAD ME DEAD TO RIGHTS! JIM, LOOK OUT!
RRAAR!

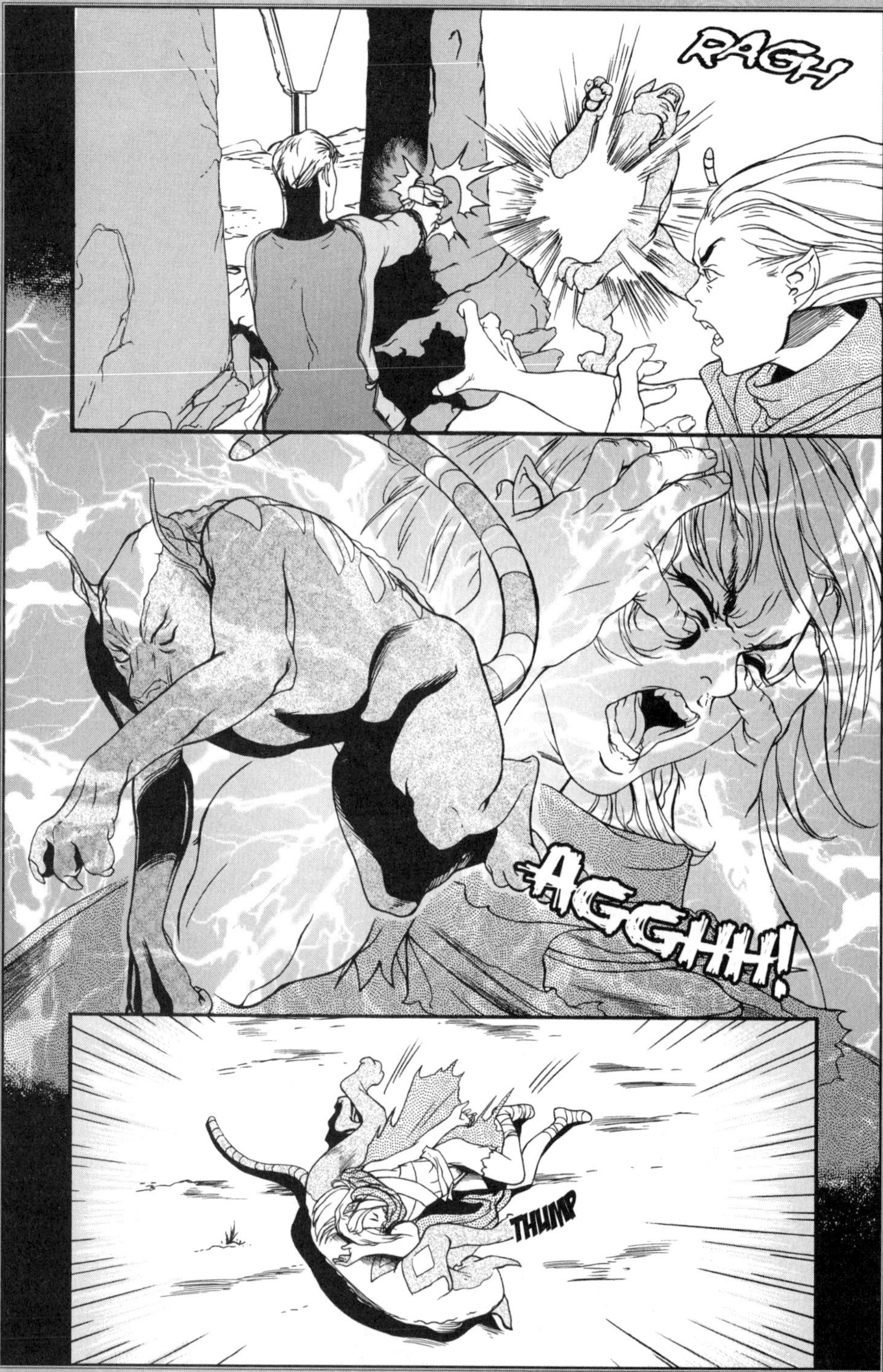
RAGH
AGGHH!
THUMP

Sneak Preview of TOKYOPOP's Star Trek the manga: Kakan ni Shinkou

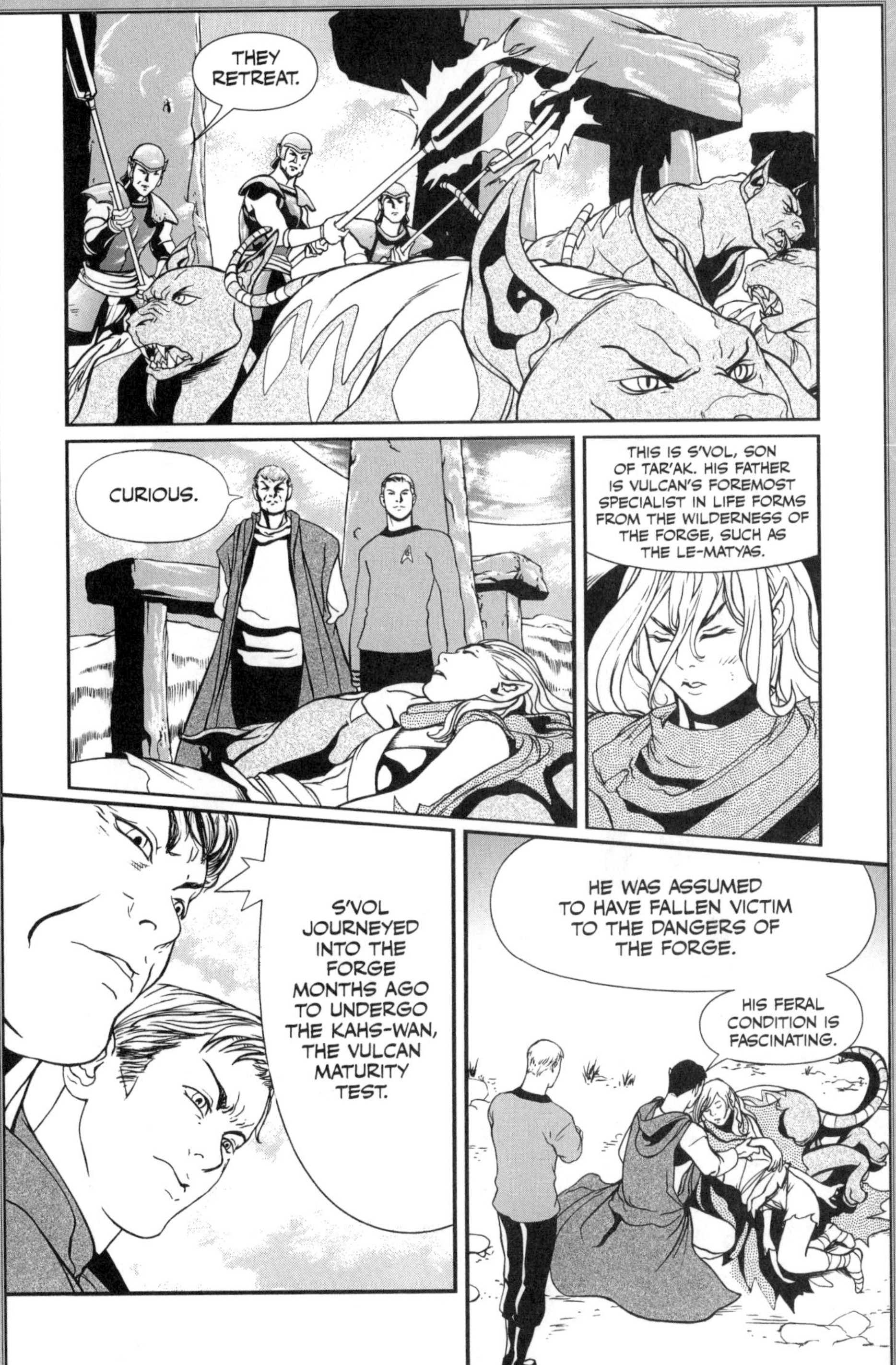
THEY RETREAT.
CURIOUS.
THIS IS S'VOL, SON OF TAR'AK. HIS FATHER IS VULCAN'S FOREMOST SPECIALIST IN LIFE FORMS FROM THE WILDERNESS OF THE FORGE, SUCH AS THE LE-MATYAS.
S'VOL JOURNEYED INTO THE FORGE MONTHS AGO TO UNDERGO THE KAHS-WAN, THE VULCAN MATURITY TEST.
HE WAS ASSUMED TO HAVE FALLEN VICTIM TO THE DANGERS OF THE FORGE.
HIS FERAL CONDITION IS FASCINATING.

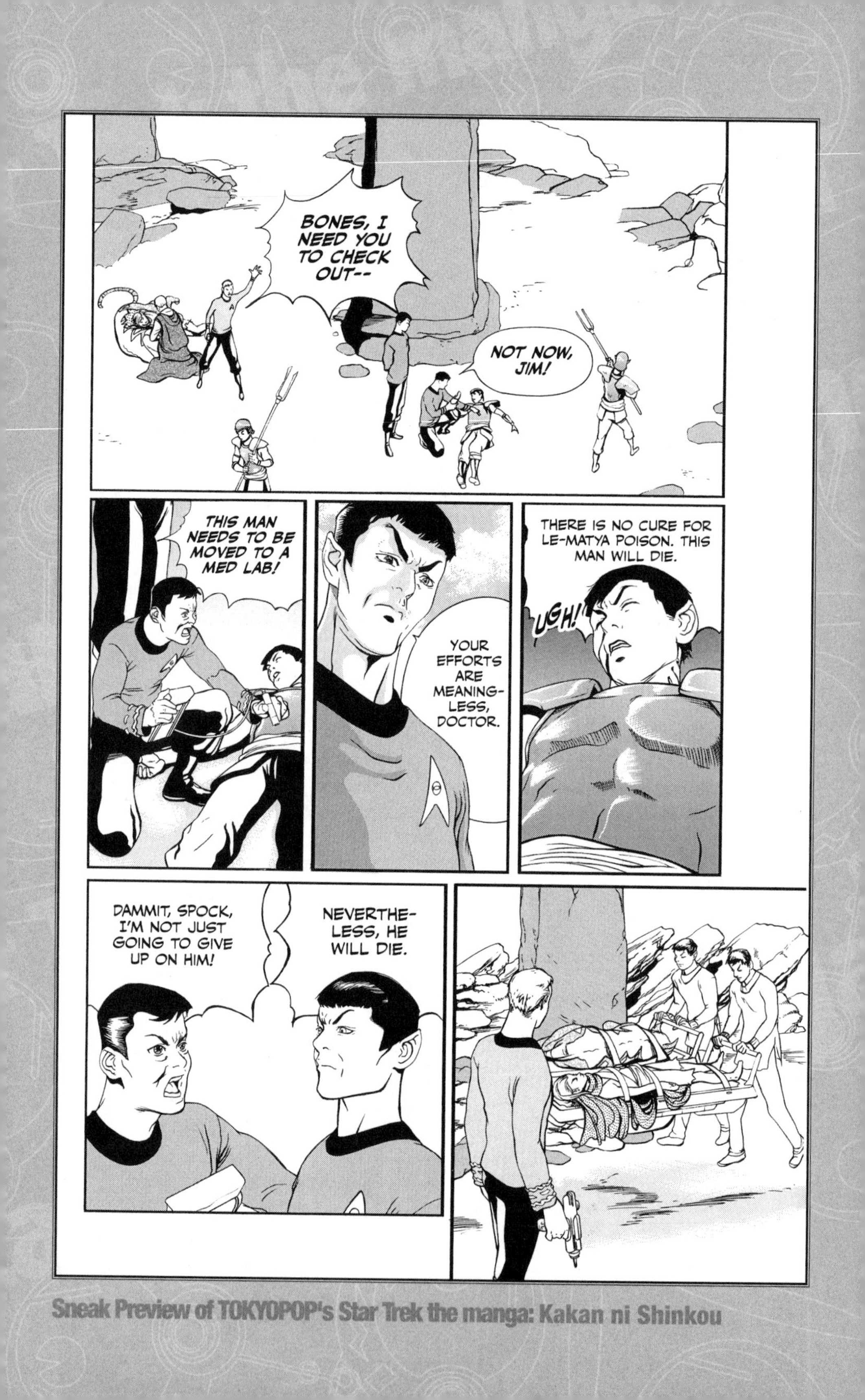
BONES, I NEED YOU TO CHECK OUT--
NOT NOW, JIM!
THIS MAN NEEDS TO BE MOVED TO A MED LAB!
YOUR EFFORTS ARE MEANING-LESS, DOCTOR.
THERE IS NO CURE FOR LE-MATYA POISON. THIS MAN WILL DIE.
UGH!
DAMMIT, SPOCK, I'M NOT JUST GOING TO GIVE UP ON HIM!
NEVERTHE-LESS, HE WILL DIE.

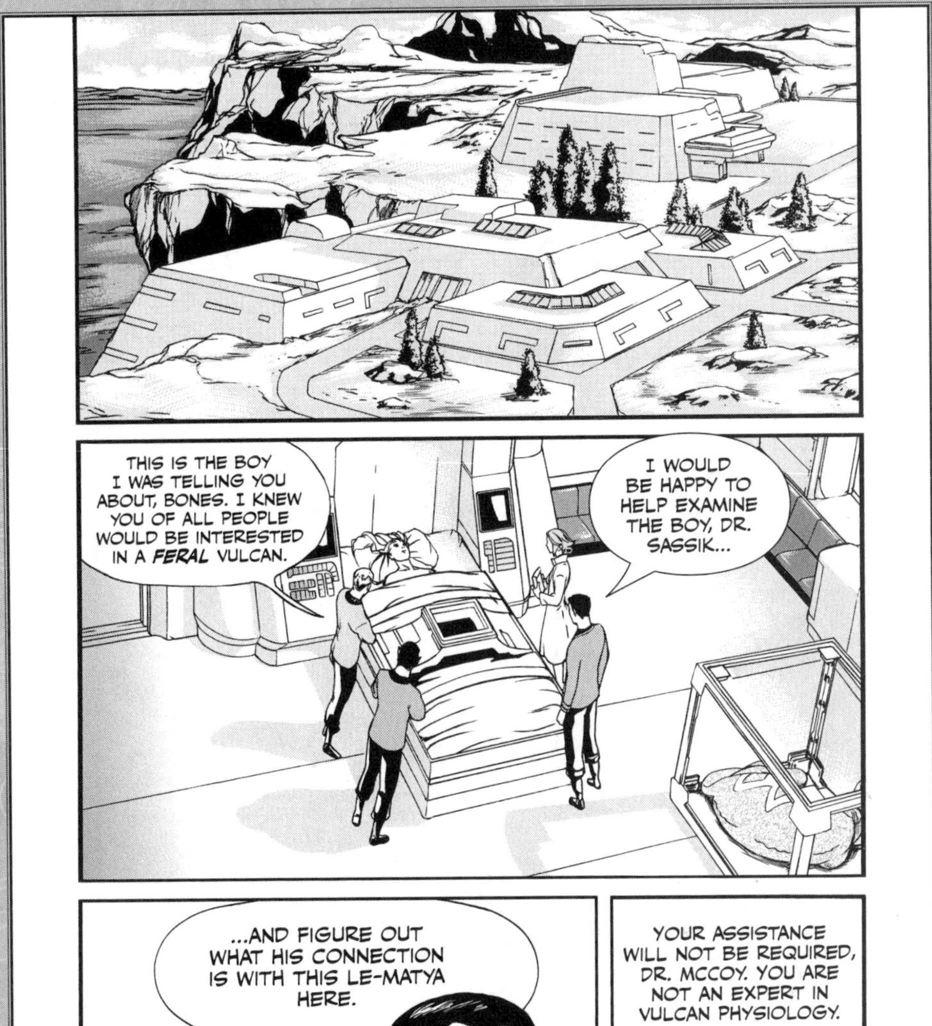
THIS IS THE BOY I WAS TELLING YOU ABOUT, BONES. I KNEW YOU OF ALL PEOPLE WOULD BE INTERESTED IN A *FERAL* VULCAN.
I WOULD BE HAPPY TO HELP EXAMINE THE BOY, DR. SASSIK...
...AND FIGURE OUT WHAT HIS CONNECTION IS WITH THIS LE-MATYA HERE.
YOUR ASSISTANCE WILL NOT BE REQUIRED, DR. MCCOY. YOU ARE NOT AN EXPERT IN VULCAN PHYSIOLOGY.

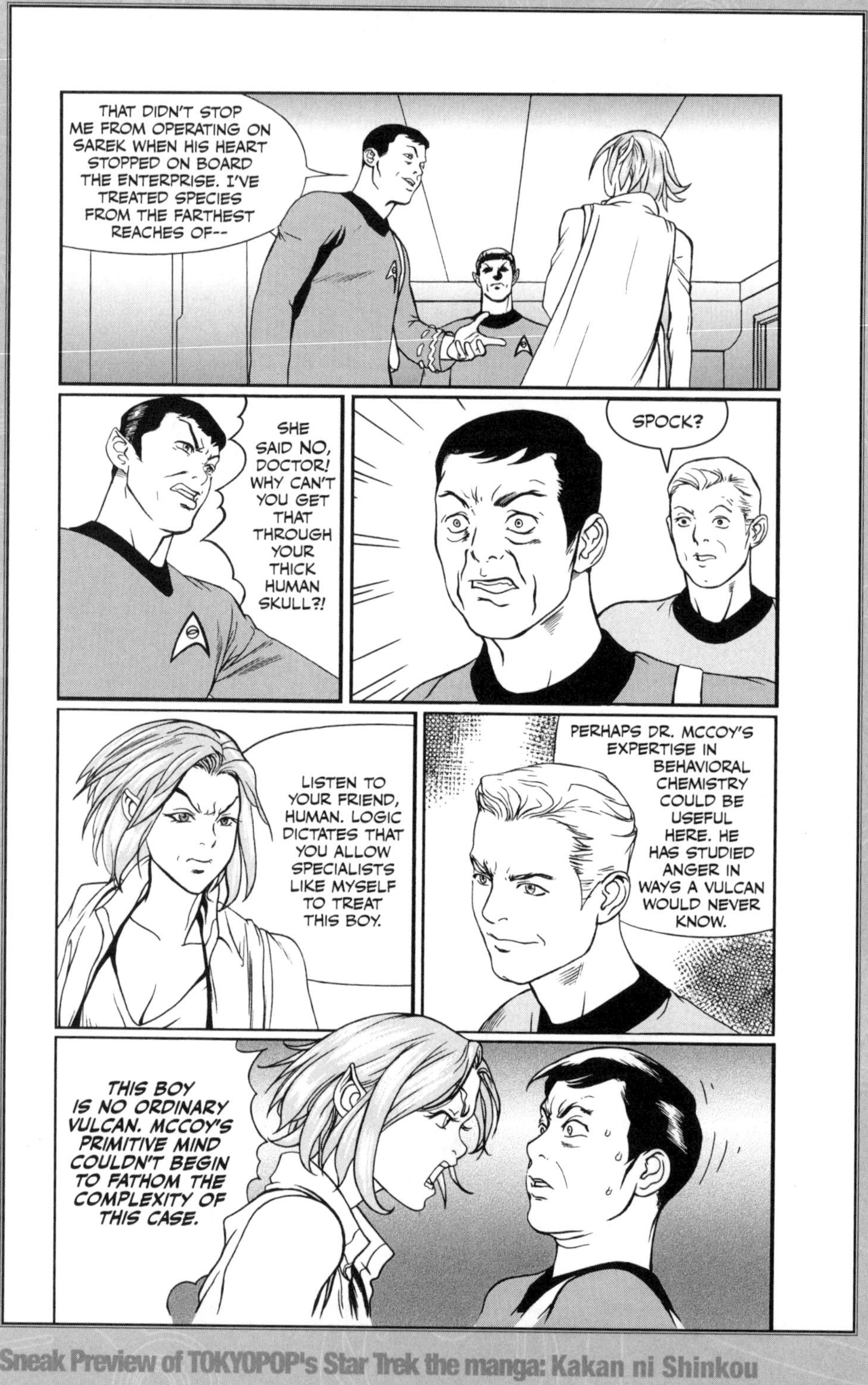
THAT DIDN'T STOP ME FROM OPERATING ON SAREK WHEN HIS HEART STOPPED ON BOARD THE ENTERPRISE. I'VE TREATED SPECIES FROM THE FARTHEST REACHES OF--
SHE SAID NO, DOCTOR! WHY CAN'T YOU GET THAT THROUGH YOUR THICK HUMAN SKULL?!
SPOCK?
LISTEN TO YOUR FRIEND, HUMAN. LOGIC DICTATES THAT YOU ALLOW SPECIALISTS LIKE MYSELF TO TREAT THIS BOY.
PERHAPS DR. MCCOY'S EXPERTISE IN BEHAVIORAL CHEMISTRY COULD BE USEFUL HERE. HE HAS STUDIED ANGER IN WAYS A VULCAN WOULD NEVER KNOW.
THIS BOY IS NO ORDINARY VULCAN. MCCOY'S PRIMITIVE MIND COULDN'T BEGIN TO FATHOM THE COMPLEXITY OF THIS CASE.

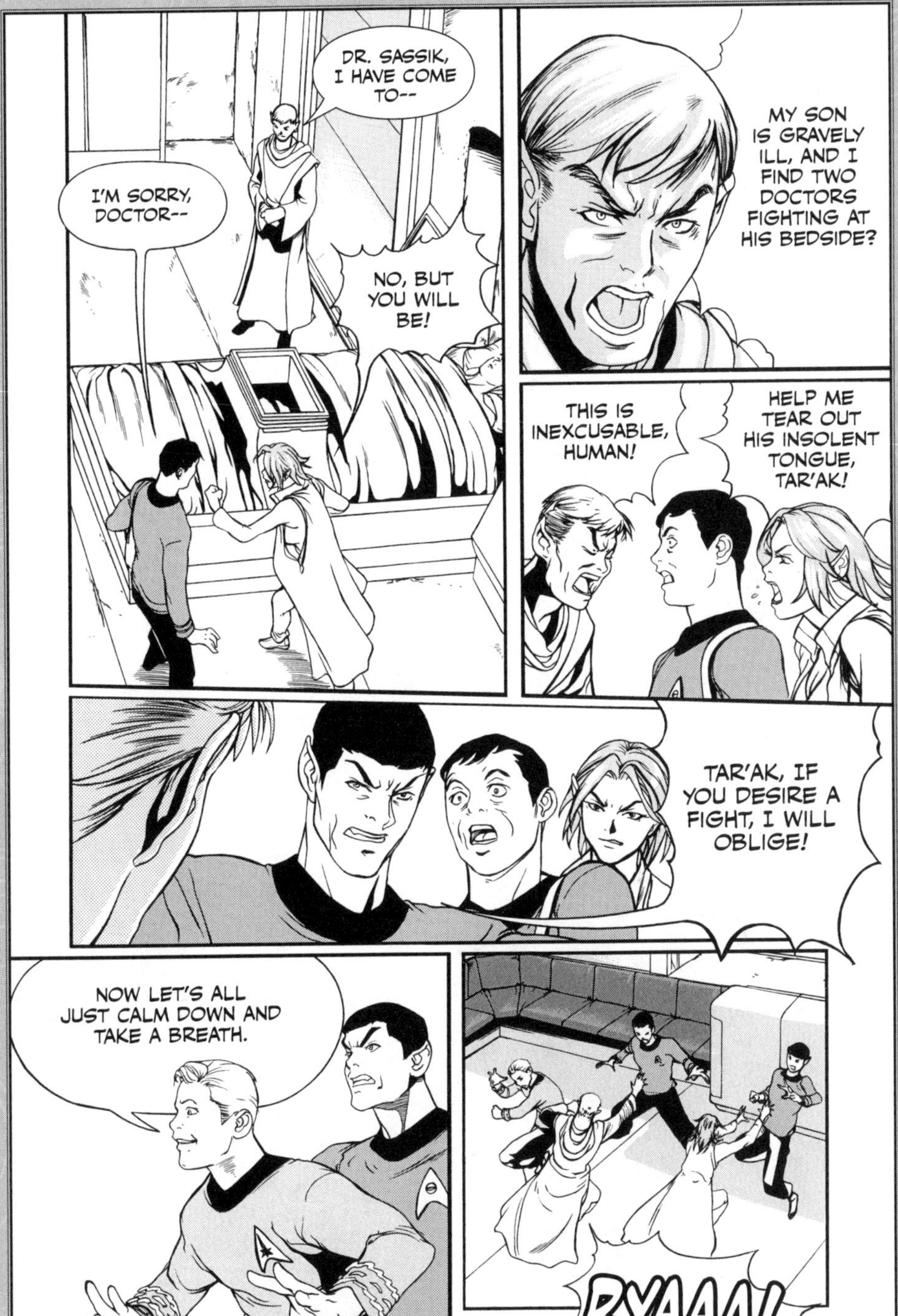
DR. SASSIK, I HAVE COME TO--
I'M SORRY, DOCTOR--
NO, BUT YOU WILL BE!
MY SON IS GRAVELY ILL, AND I FIND TWO DOCTORS FIGHTING AT HIS BEDSIDE?
THIS IS INEXCUSABLE, HUMAN!
HELP ME TEAR OUT HIS INSOLENT TONGUE, TAR'AK!
TAR'AK, IF YOU DESIRE A FIGHT, I WILL OBLIGE!
NOW LET'S ALL JUST CALM DOWN AND TAKE A BREATH.
RYAAA!

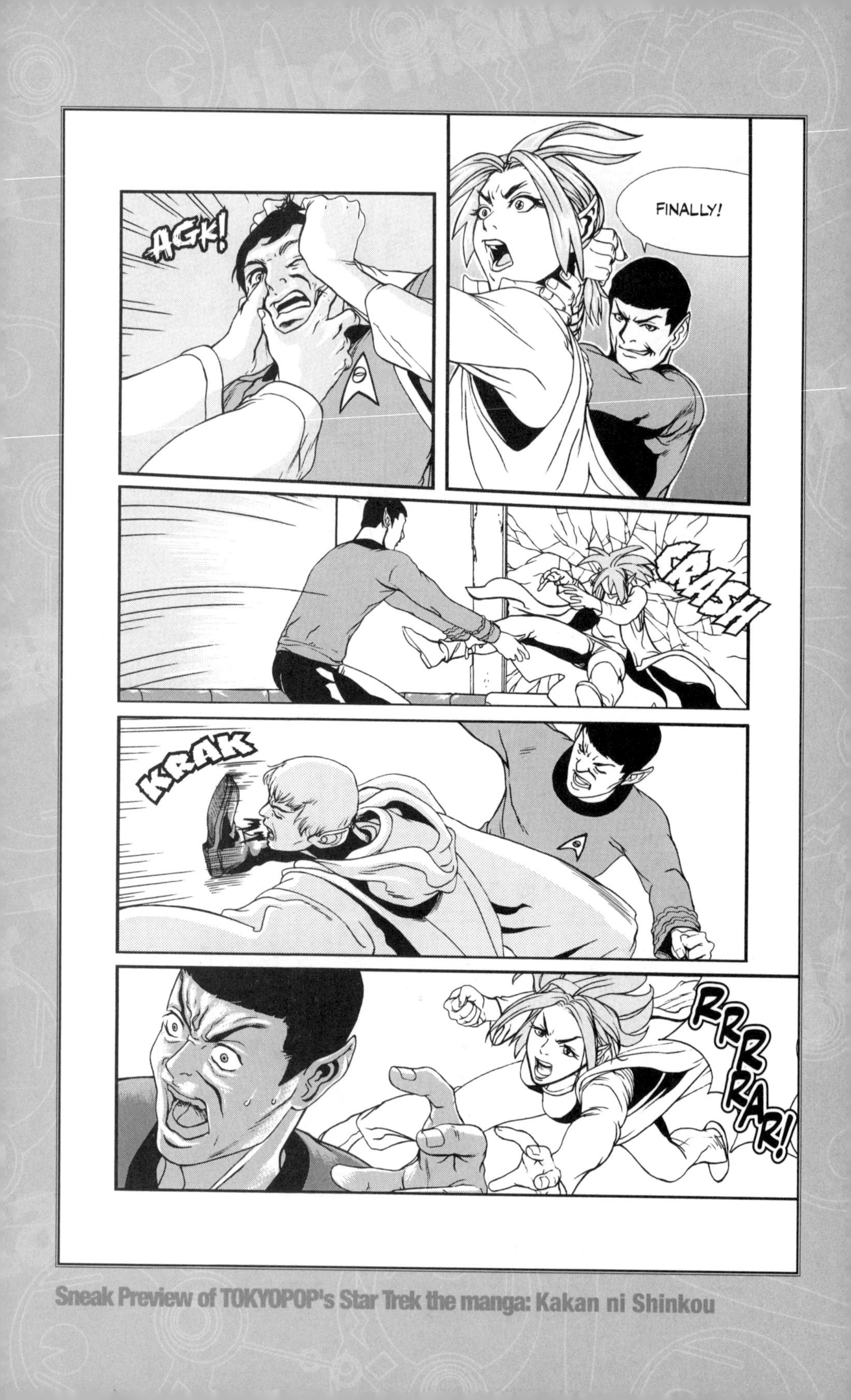
AGK!
FINALLY!
CRASH
KRAK
RRRRAR!

Sneak Preview of TOKYOPOP's Star Trek the manga: Kakan ni Shinkou

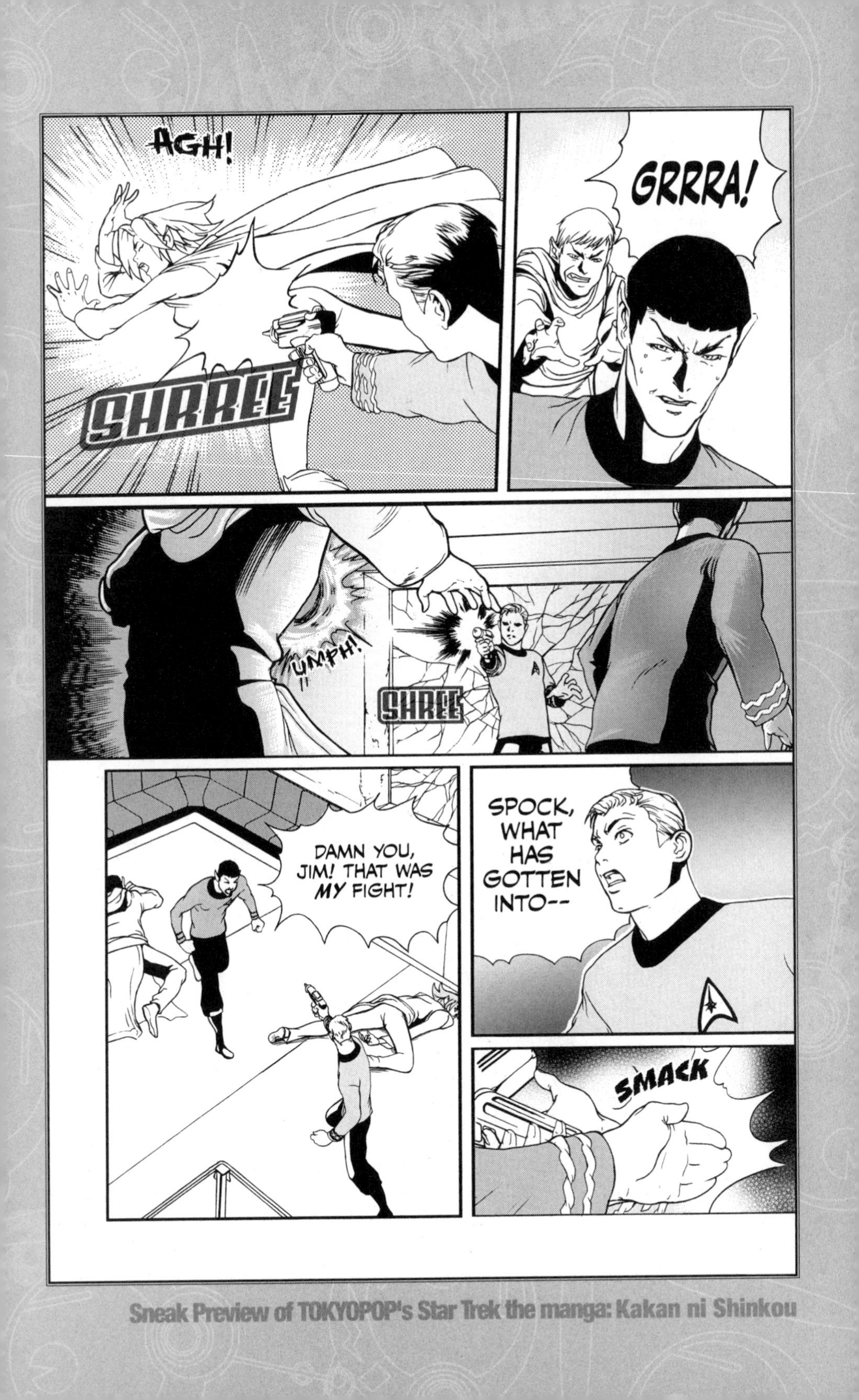
AGH!
SHREE
GRRRA!
UMPH!
SHREE
DAMN YOU, JIM! THAT WAS *MY* FIGHT!
SPOCK, WHAT HAS GOTTEN INTO--
SMACK

Sneak Preview of TOKYOPOP's Star Trek the manga: Kakan ni Shinkou

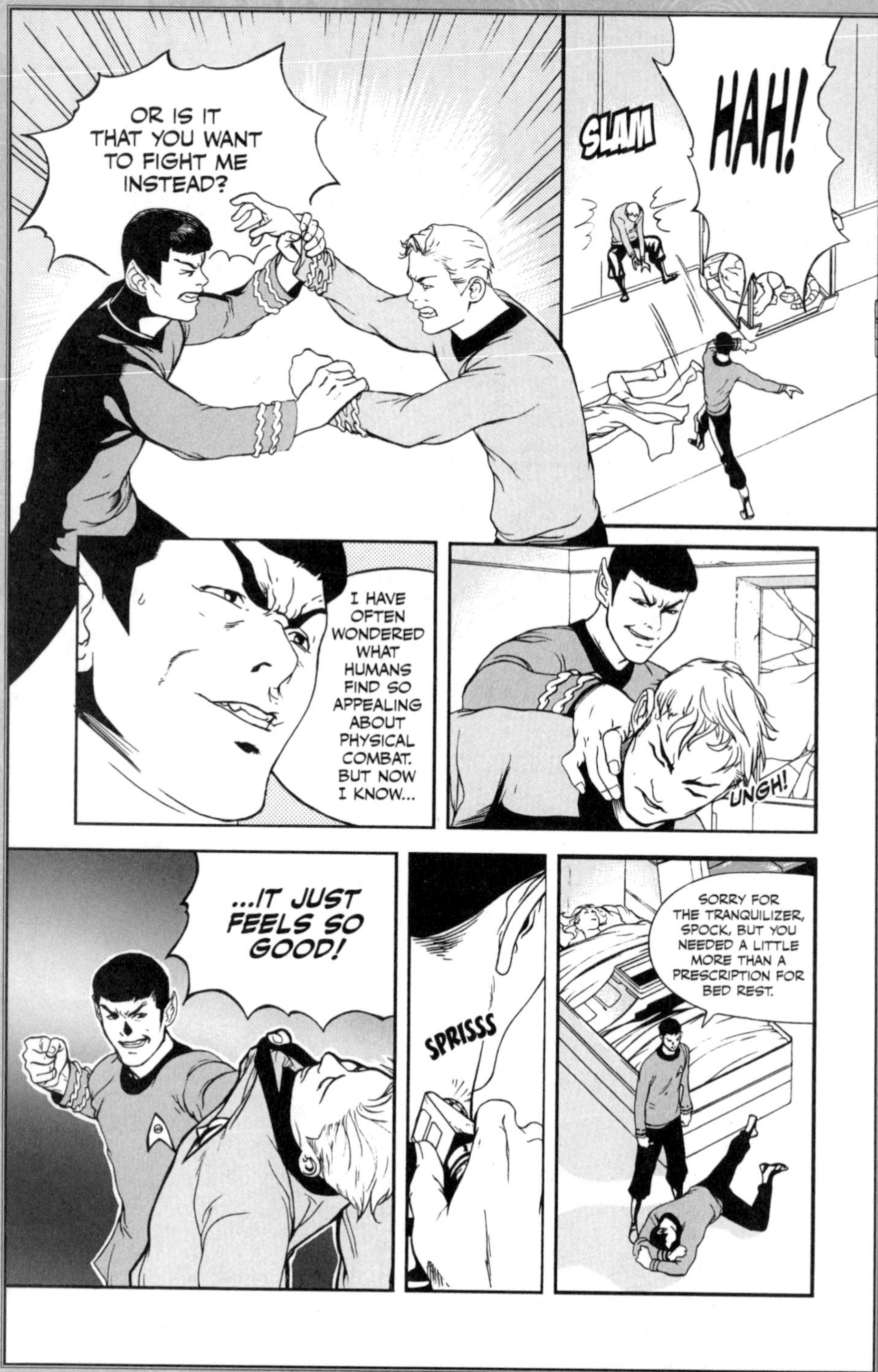
OR IS IT THAT YOU WANT TO FIGHT ME INSTEAD?
SLAM
HAH!
I HAVE OFTEN WONDERED WHAT HUMANS FIND SO APPEALING ABOUT PHYSICAL COMBAT. BUT NOW I KNOW...
UNGH!
...IT JUST FEELS SO GOOD!
SPRISSS
SORRY FOR THE TRANQUILIZER, SPOCK, BUT YOU NEEDED A LITTLE MORE THAN A PRESCRIPTION FOR BED REST.

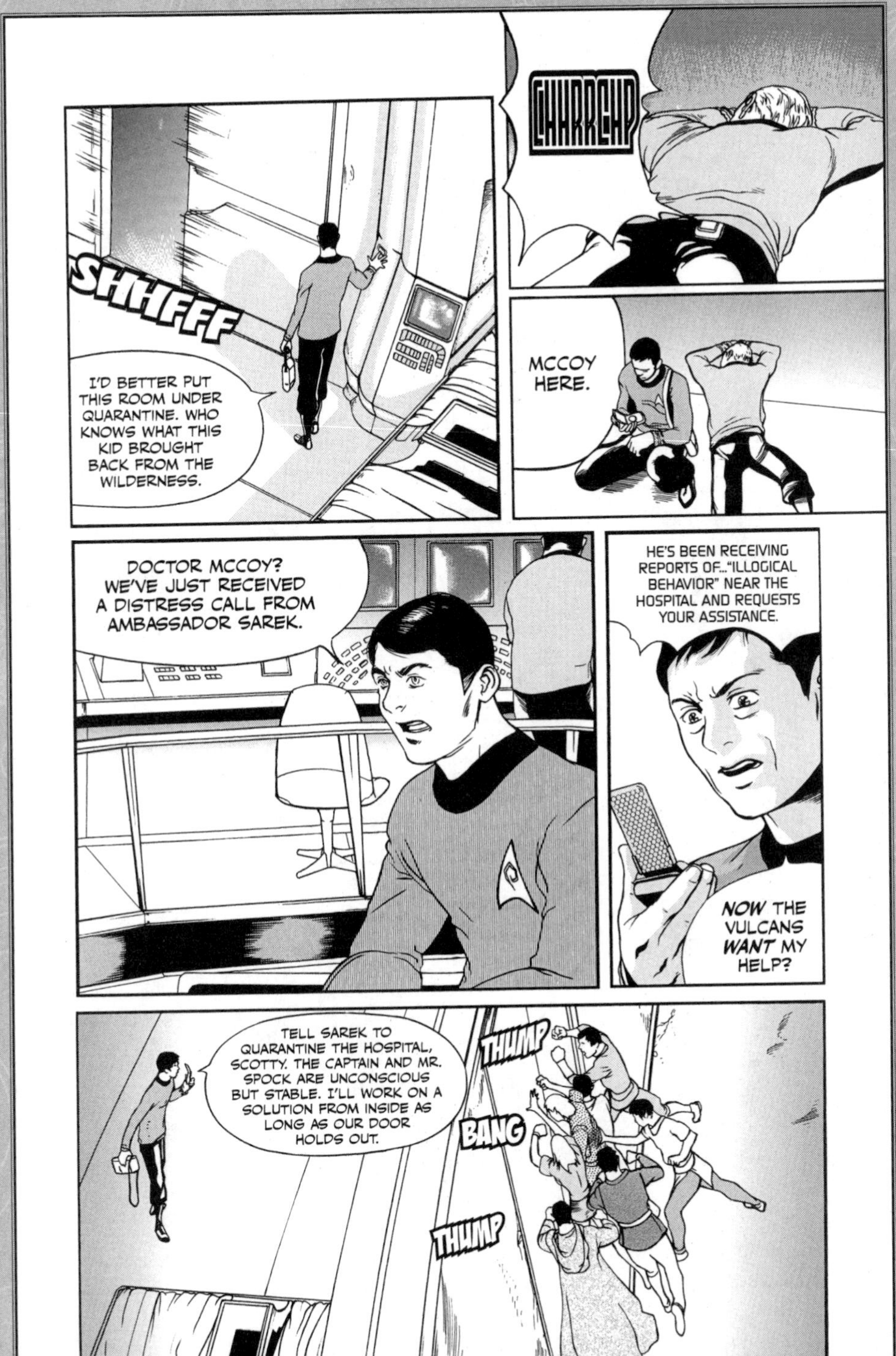
SHHFFF
I'D BETTER PUT THIS ROOM UNDER QUARANTINE. WHO KNOWS WHAT THIS KID BROUGHT BACK FROM THE WILDERNESS.
CHHRRCHP
MCCOY HERE.
DOCTOR MCCOY? WE'VE JUST RECEIVED A DISTRESS CALL FROM AMBASSADOR SAREK.
HE'S BEEN RECEIVING REPORTS OF..."ILLOGICAL BEHAVIOR" NEAR THE HOSPITAL AND REQUESTS YOUR ASSISTANCE.
NOW THE VULCANS *WANT* MY HELP?
TELL SAREK TO QUARANTINE THE HOSPITAL, SCOTTY. THE CAPTAIN AND MR. SPOCK ARE UNCONSCIOUS BUT STABLE. I'LL WORK ON A SOLUTION FROM INSIDE AS LONG AS OUR DOOR HOLDS OUT.
THUMP
BANG
THUMP

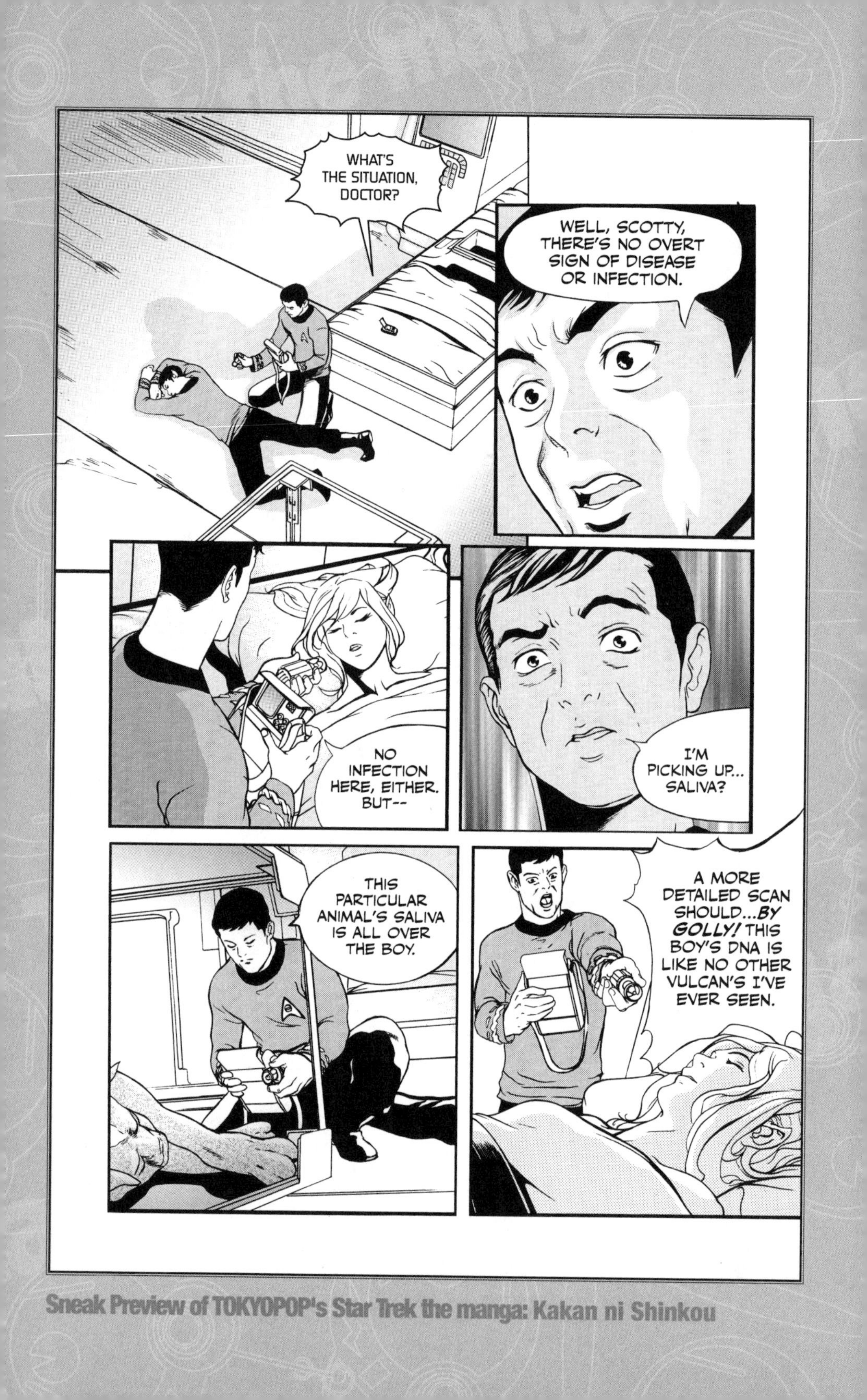
WHAT'S THE SITUATION, DOCTOR?
WELL, SCOTTY, THERE'S NO OVERT SIGN OF DISEASE OR INFECTION.
NO INFECTION HERE, EITHER. BUT--
I'M PICKING UP... SALIVA?
THIS PARTICULAR ANIMAL'S SALIVA IS ALL OVER THE BOY.
A MORE DETAILED SCAN SHOULD... *BY GOLLY!* THIS BOY'S DNA IS LIKE NO OTHER VULCAN'S I'VE EVER SEEN.

Sneak Preview of TOKYOPOP's Star Trek the manga: Kakan ni Shinkou

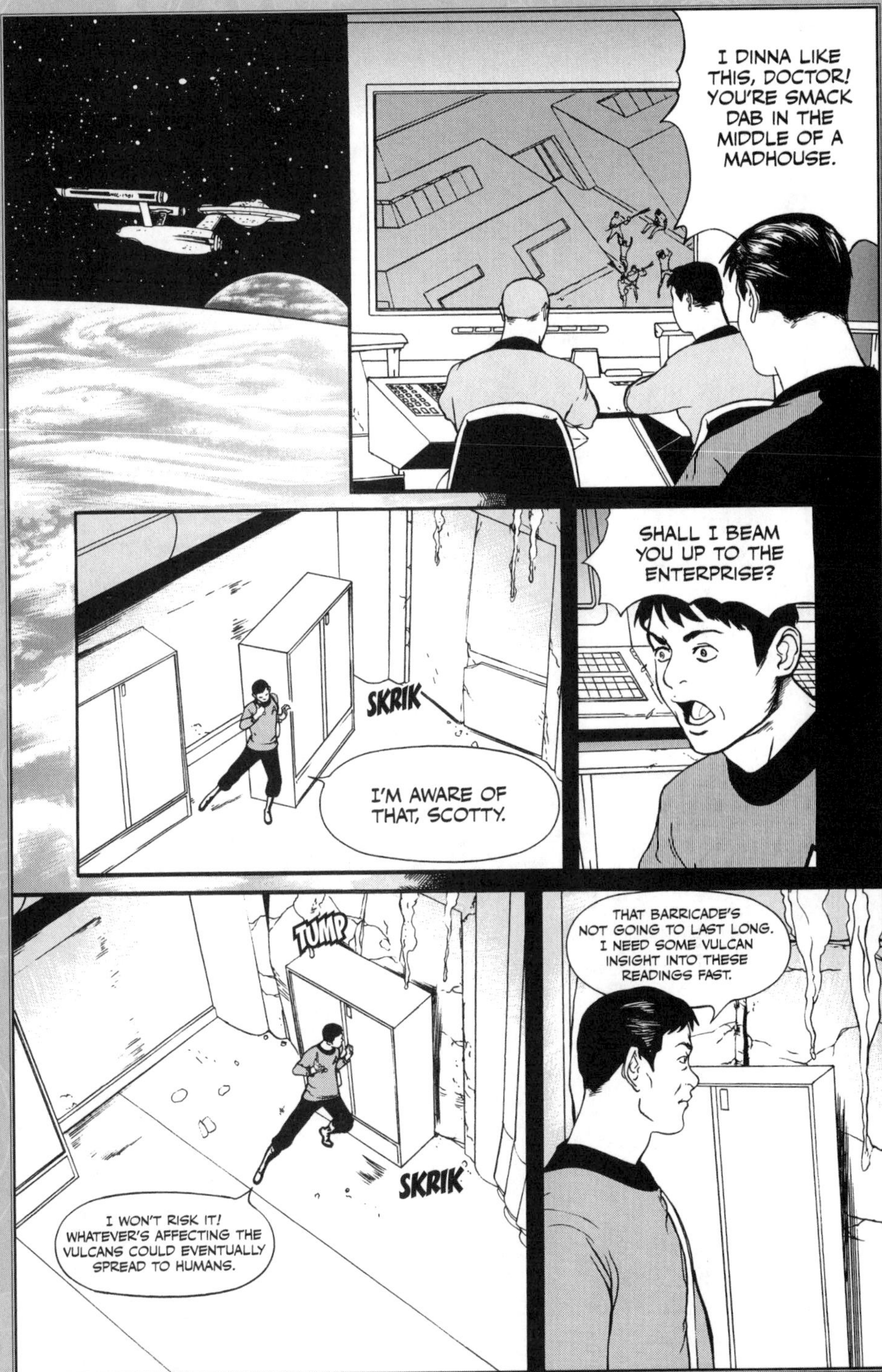
I DINNA LIKE THIS, DOCTOR! YOU'RE SMACK DAB IN THE MIDDLE OF A MADHOUSE.
SKRIK
I'M AWARE OF THAT, SCOTTY.
SHALL I BEAM YOU UP TO THE ENTERPRISE?
TUMP
SKRIK
I WON'T RISK IT! WHATEVER'S AFFECTING THE VULCANS COULD EVENTUALLY SPREAD TO HUMANS.
THAT BARRICADE'S NOT GOING TO LAST LONG. I NEED SOME VULCAN INSIGHT INTO THESE READINGS FAST.

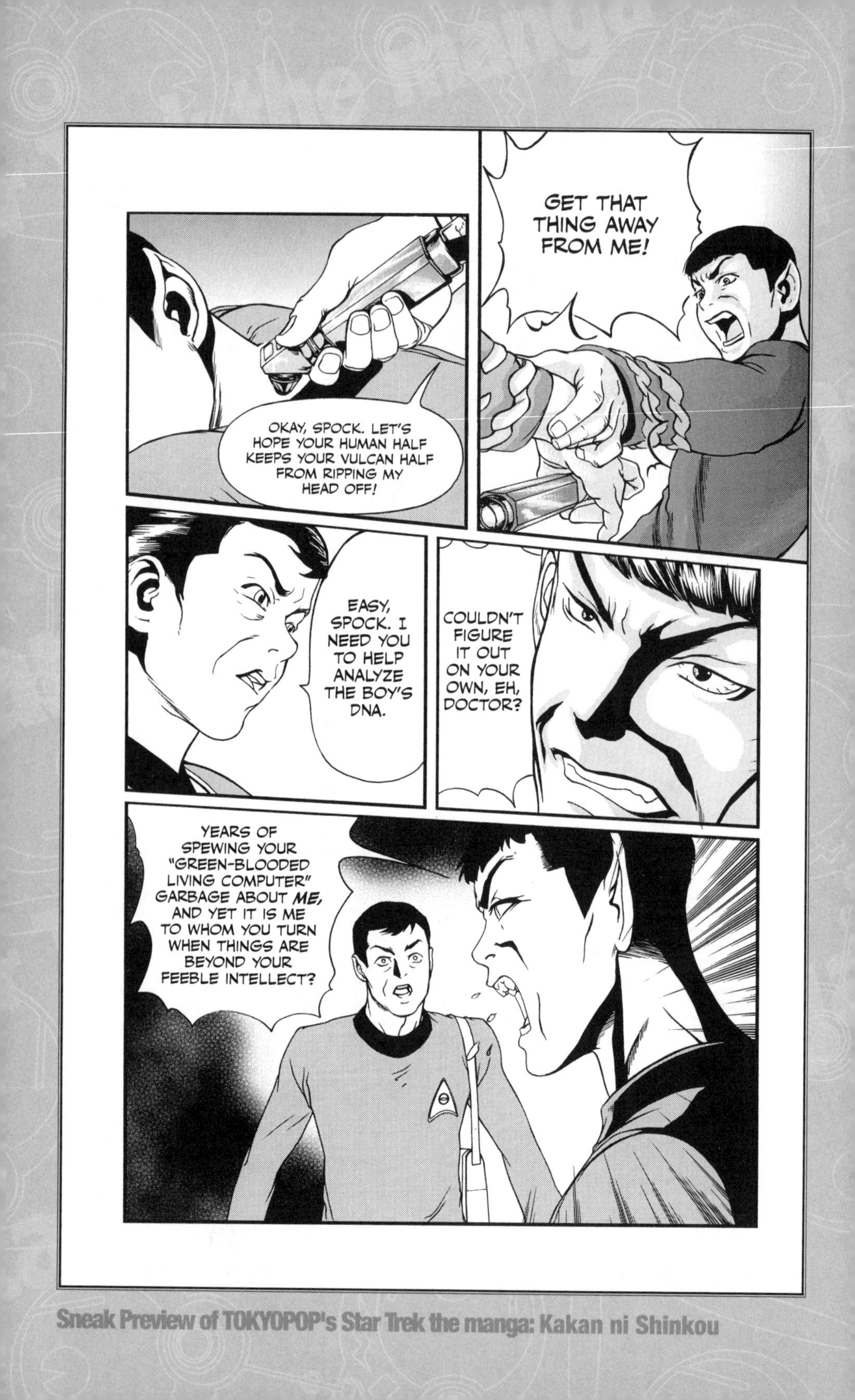
OKAY, SPOCK. LET'S HOPE YOUR HUMAN HALF KEEPS YOUR VULCAN HALF FROM RIPPING MY HEAD OFF!
GET THAT THING AWAY FROM ME!
EASY, SPOCK. I NEED YOU TO HELP ANALYZE THE BOY'S DNA.
COULDN'T FIGURE IT OUT ON YOUR OWN, EH, DOCTOR?
YEARS OF SPEWING YOUR "GREEN-BLOODED LIVING COMPUTER" GARBAGE ABOUT *ME*, AND YET IT IS ME TO WHOM YOU TURN WHEN THINGS ARE BEYOND YOUR FEEBLE INTELLECT?

SNATCH

IT SHOULD BE OBVIOUS EVEN TO YOU THAT HIS DNA HAS BEEN ALTERED AT A FUNDAMENTAL LEVEL.

YES, THE DONOR DNA WAS GRAFTED ON SOME TIME AGO, BUT I'VE NEVER SEEN THOSE PATTERNS BEFORE.

THAT'S BECAUSE YOU'RE TOO SELF-RIGHTEOUS TO LEARN MORE ABOUT THE PLANET VULCAN. THIS DNA IS A COMPOSITE OF LIFE FORMS NATIVE TO THE FORGE.

SELF-RIGHTEOUS?! YOU'RE THE ONE WHO'S ALWAYS ACTING LIKE HE'S BETTER THAN THE REST OF US!

UGH!

IF IT WERE MERELY ACTING, YOU WOULDN'T NEED MY HELP.

I THINK I LIKED YOU BETTER WHEN YOU WERE AN UNFEELING COMPUTER.

MORE ANTI-VULCAN SENTIMENT! HOW DO YOU THINK THAT MAKES ME FEEL?

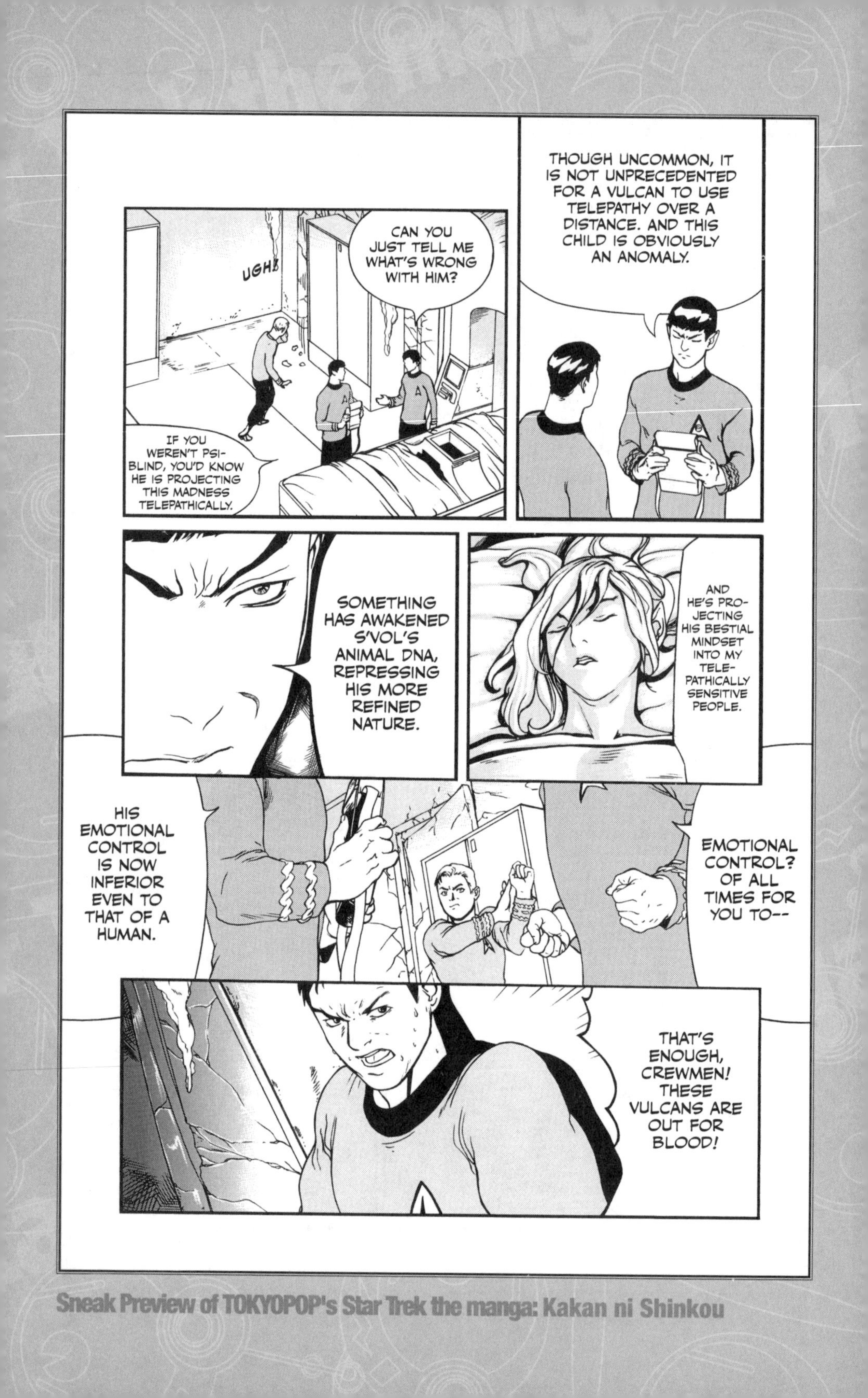
UGH
CAN YOU JUST TELL ME WHAT'S WRONG WITH HIM?
IF YOU WEREN'T PSI-BLIND, YOU'D KNOW HE IS PROJECTING THIS MADNESS TELEPATHICALLY.
THOUGH UNCOMMON, IT IS NOT UNPRECEDENTED FOR A VULCAN TO USE TELEPATHY OVER A DISTANCE. AND THIS CHILD IS OBVIOUSLY AN ANOMALY.
SOMETHING HAS AWAKENED S'VOL'S ANIMAL DNA, REPRESSING HIS MORE REFINED NATURE.
AND HE'S PRO-JECTING HIS BESTIAL MINDSET INTO MY TELE-PATHICALLY SENSITIVE PEOPLE.
HIS EMOTIONAL CONTROL IS NOW INFERIOR EVEN TO THAT OF A HUMAN.
EMOTIONAL CONTROL? OF ALL TIMES FOR YOU TO--
THAT'S ENOUGH, CREWMEN! THESE VULCANS ARE OUT FOR BLOOD!

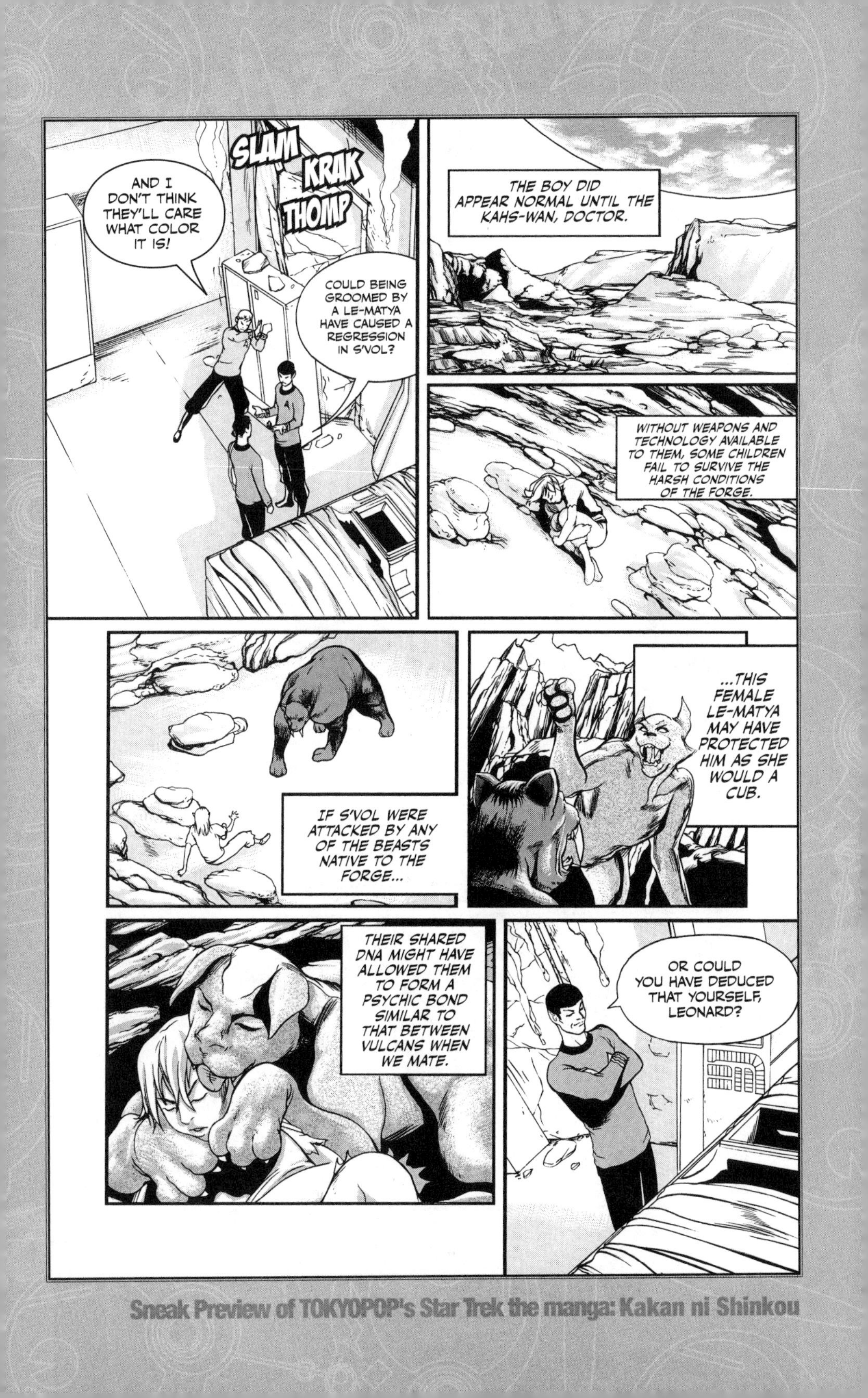
SLAM
KRAK
THOMP
AND I DON'T THINK THEY'LL CARE WHAT COLOR IT IS!
COULD BEING GROOMED BY A LE-MATYA HAVE CAUSED A REGRESSION IN S'VOL?
THE BOY DID APPEAR NORMAL UNTIL THE KAHS-WAN, DOCTOR.
WITHOUT WEAPONS AND TECHNOLOGY AVAILABLE TO THEM, SOME CHILDREN FAIL TO SURVIVE THE HARSH CONDITIONS OF THE FORGE.
IF S'VOL WERE ATTACKED BY ANY OF THE BEASTS NATIVE TO THE FORGE...
...THIS FEMALE LE-MATYA MAY HAVE PROTECTED HIM AS SHE WOULD A CUB.
THEIR SHARED DNA MIGHT HAVE ALLOWED THEM TO FORM A PSYCHIC BOND SIMILAR TO THAT BETWEEN VULCANS WHEN WE MATE.
OR COULD YOU HAVE DEDUCED THAT YOURSELF, LEONARD?

Sneak Preview of TOKYOPOP's Star Trek the manga: Kakan ni Shinkou

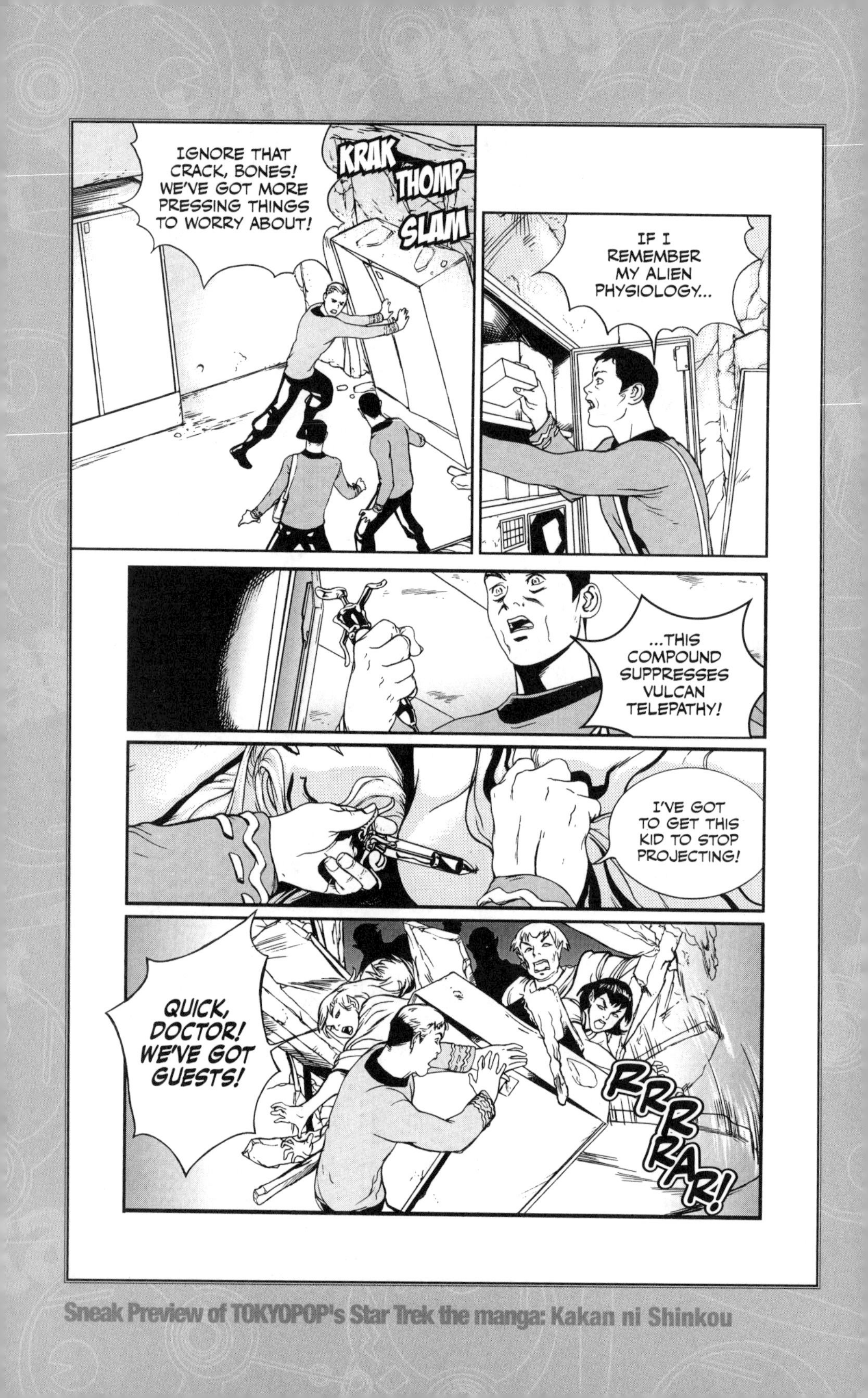
IGNORE THAT CRACK, BONES! WE'VE GOT MORE PRESSING THINGS TO WORRY ABOUT!
KRAK
THOMP
SLAM
IF I REMEMBER MY ALIEN PHYSIOLOGY...
...THIS COMPOUND SUPPRESSES VULCAN TELEPATHY!
I'VE GOT TO GET THIS KID TO STOP PROJECTING!
QUICK, DOCTOR! WE'VE GOT GUESTS!
RRRRAR!

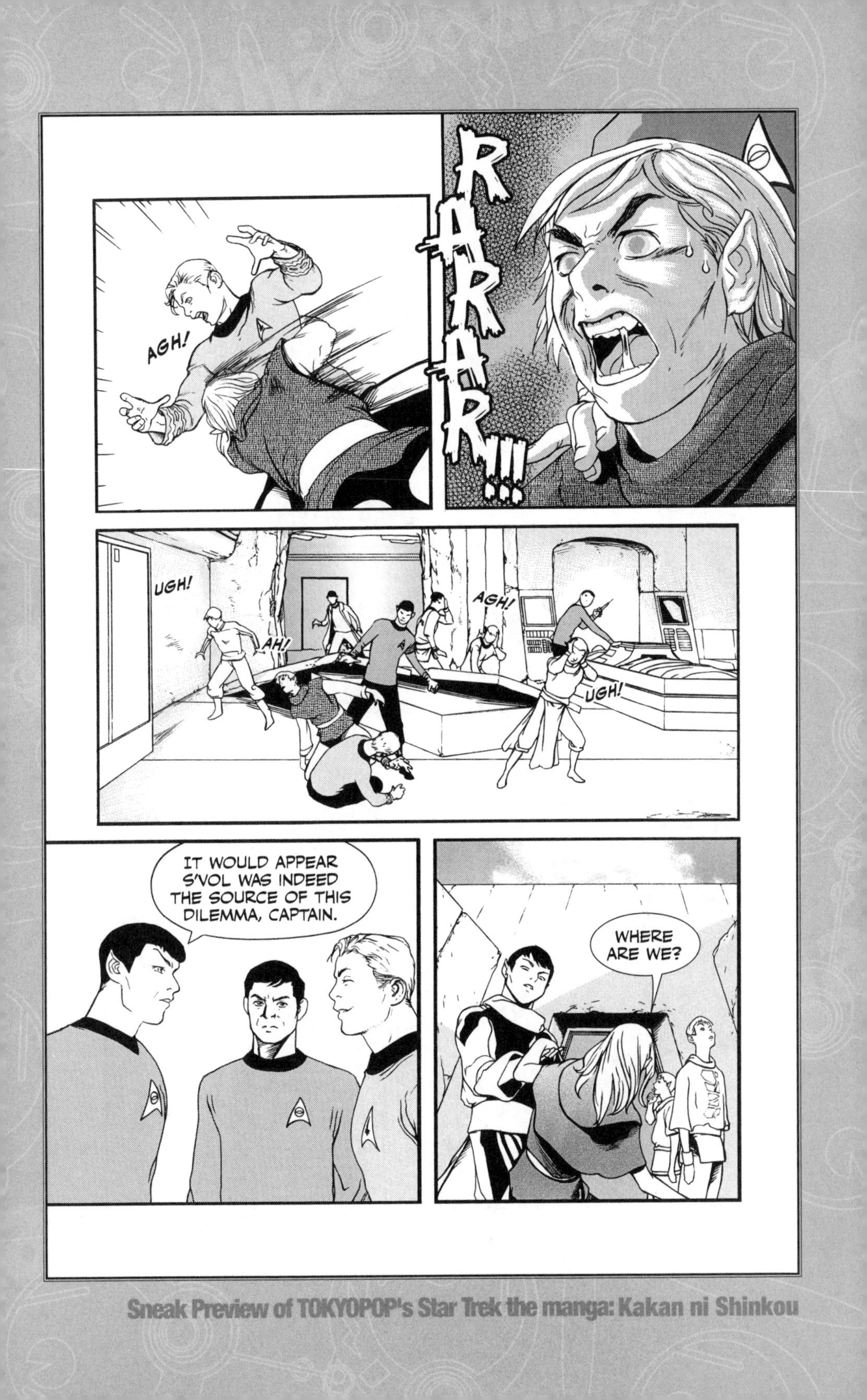
AGH!
RARAR!!!
UGH!
AH!
AGH!
UGH!
IT WOULD APPEAR S'VOL WAS INDEED THE SOURCE OF THIS DILEMMA, CAPTAIN.
WHERE ARE WE?

I APOLOGIZE FOR MY WEAKNESS EARLIER, CAPTAIN.
IF WE SPENT ALL OUR TIME APOLOGIZING FOR WEAKNESS, MR. SPOCK, WE'D NEVER GET ANYTHING DONE.
I AM A VULCAN. LOSING CONTROL OF MYSELF IS... REGRETTABLE.
YOU RETAINED MORE CONTROL THAN YOUR FELLOW VULCANS, SPOCK.
I SUSPECT THAT MAY HAVE MORE TO DO WITH MY HUMAN HERITAGE THAN MY SELF-CONTROL, CAPTAIN.
WE SHOULD RETURN THIS LE-MATYA TO THE FORGE. THE GREATER THE DISTANCE BETWEEN THE BEAST AND S'VOL, THE LESS LIKELY THEY ARE TO RE-FORM THEIR BOND.
VERY WELL. I'LL SEE TO IT.

Sneak Preview of TOKYOPOP's Star Trek the manga: Kakan ni Shinkou

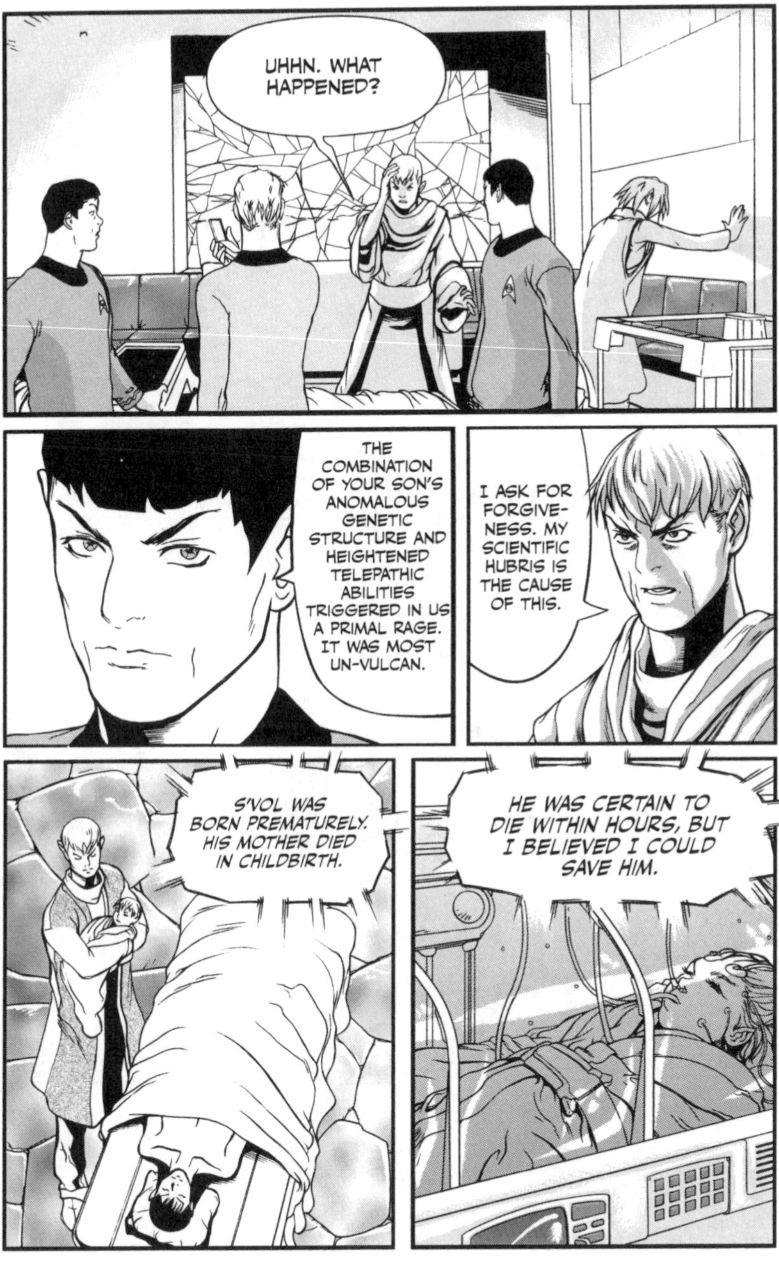
UHHN. WHAT HAPPENED?
THE COMBINATION OF YOUR SON'S ANOMALOUS GENETIC STRUCTURE AND HEIGHTENED TELEPATHIC ABILITIES TRIGGERED IN US A PRIMAL RAGE. IT WAS MOST UN-VULCAN.
I ASK FOR FORGIVE-NESS. MY SCIENTIFIC HUBRIS IS THE CAUSE OF THIS.
S'VOL WAS BORN PREMATURELY. HIS MOTHER DIED IN CHILDBIRTH.
HE WAS CERTAIN TO DIE WITHIN HOURS, BUT I BELIEVED I COULD SAVE HIM.

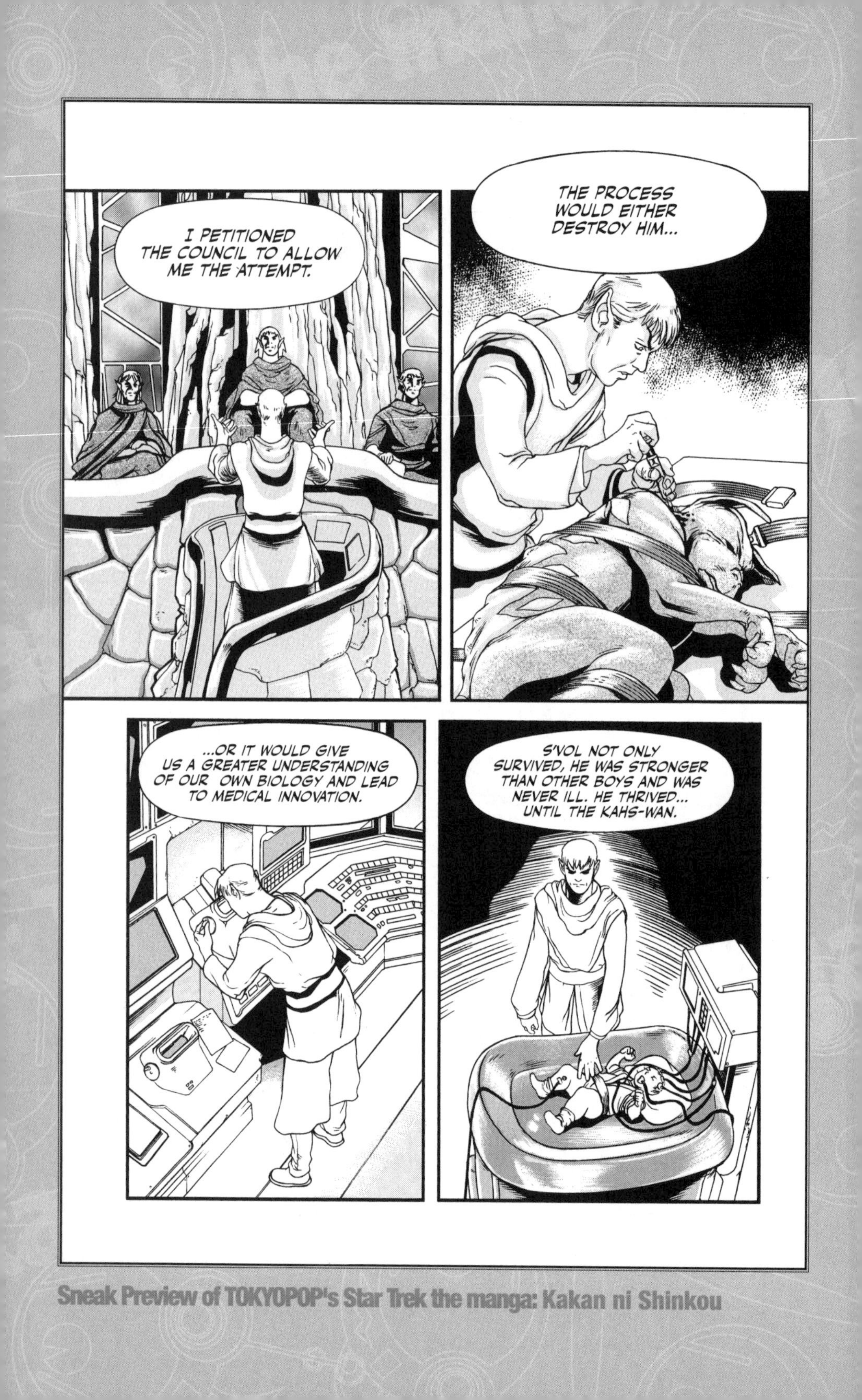
I PETITIONED THE COUNCIL TO ALLOW ME THE ATTEMPT.
THE PROCESS WOULD EITHER DESTROY HIM...
...OR IT WOULD GIVE US A GREATER UNDERSTANDING OF OUR OWN BIOLOGY AND LEAD TO MEDICAL INNOVATION.
S'VOL NOT ONLY SURVIVED, HE WAS STRONGER THAN OTHER BOYS AND WAS NEVER ILL. HE THRIVED... UNTIL THE KAHS-WAN.

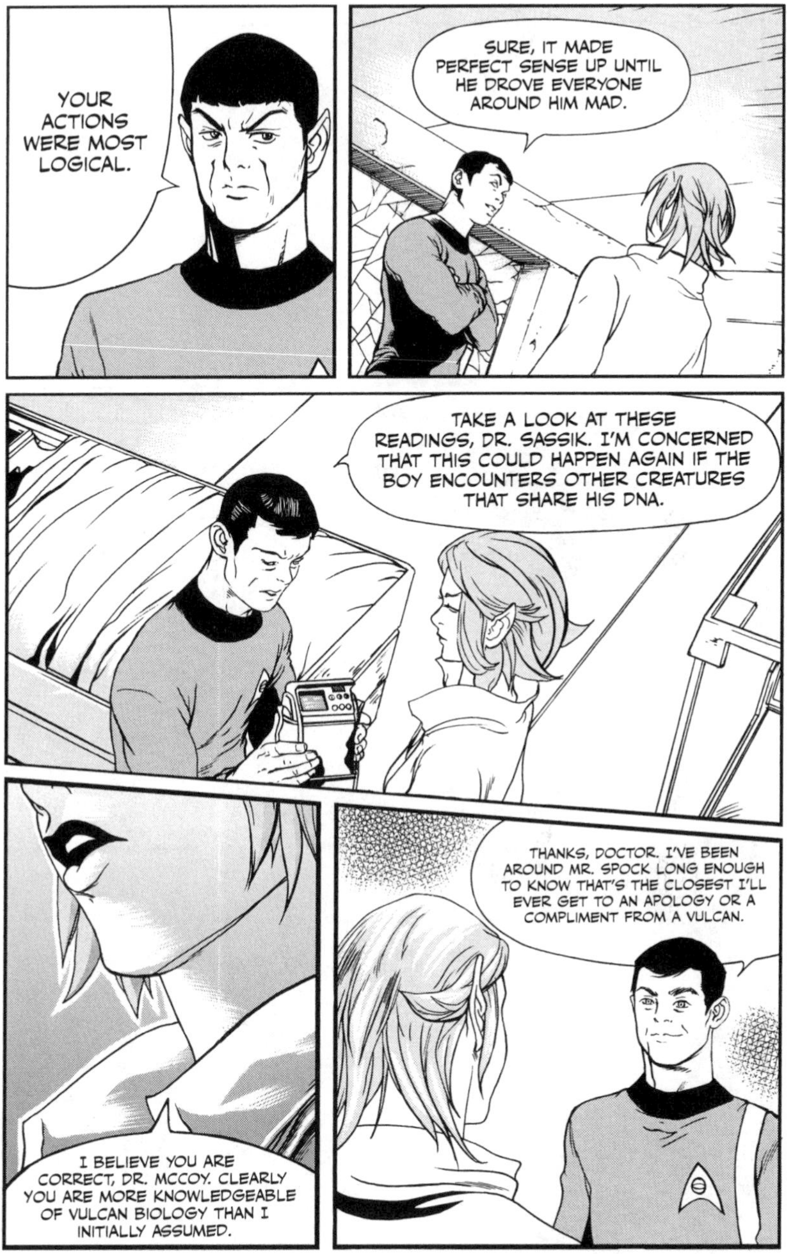
YOUR ACTIONS WERE MOST LOGICAL.
SURE, IT MADE PERFECT SENSE UP UNTIL HE DROVE EVERYONE AROUND HIM MAD.
TAKE A LOOK AT THESE READINGS, DR. SASSIK. I'M CONCERNED THAT THIS COULD HAPPEN AGAIN IF THE BOY ENCOUNTERS OTHER CREATURES THAT SHARE HIS DNA.
I BELIEVE YOU ARE CORRECT, DR. MCCOY. CLEARLY YOU ARE MORE KNOWLEDGEABLE OF VULCAN BIOLOGY THAN I INITIALLY ASSUMED.
THANKS, DOCTOR. I'VE BEEN AROUND MR. SPOCK LONG ENOUGH TO KNOW THAT'S THE CLOSEST I'LL EVER GET TO AN APOLOGY OR A COMPLIMENT FROM A VULCAN.

Sneak Preview of TOKYOPOP's Star Trek the manga: Kakan ni Shinkou

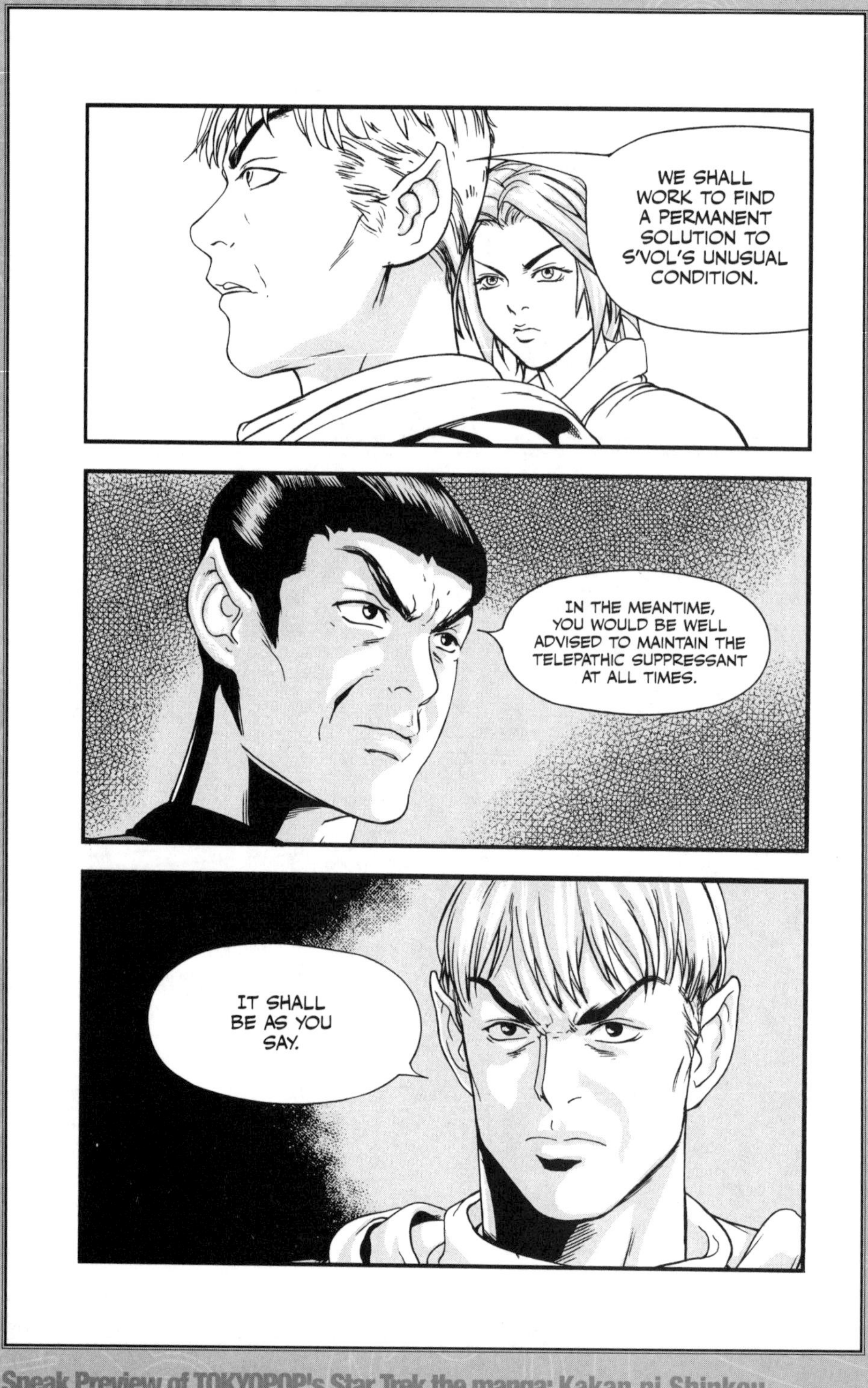
WE SHALL WORK TO FIND A PERMANENT SOLUTION TO S'VOL'S UNUSUAL CONDITION.
IN THE MEANTIME, YOU WOULD BE WELL ADVISED TO MAINTAIN THE TELEPATHIC SUPPRESSANT AT ALL TIMES.
IT SHALL BE AS YOU SAY.

Sneak Preview of TOKYOPOP's Star Trek the manga: Kakan ni Shinkou

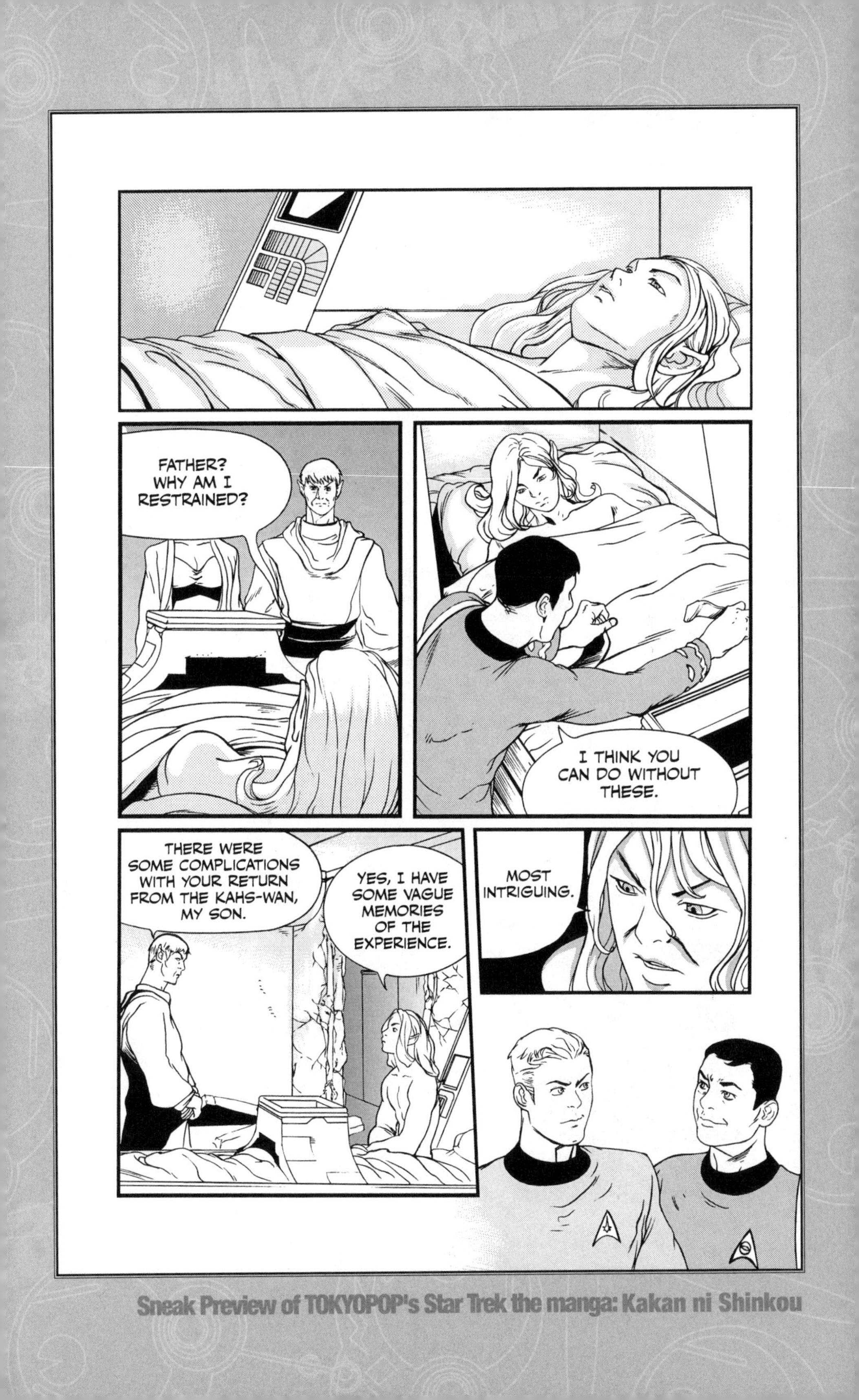
FATHER? WHY AM I RESTRAINED?
I THINK YOU CAN DO WITHOUT THESE.
THERE WERE SOME COMPLICATIONS WITH YOUR RETURN FROM THE KAHS-WAN, MY SON.
YES, I HAVE SOME VAGUE MEMORIES OF THE EXPERIENCE.
MOST INTRIGUING.

Sneak Preview of TOKYOPOP's Star Trek the manga: Kakan ni Shinkou

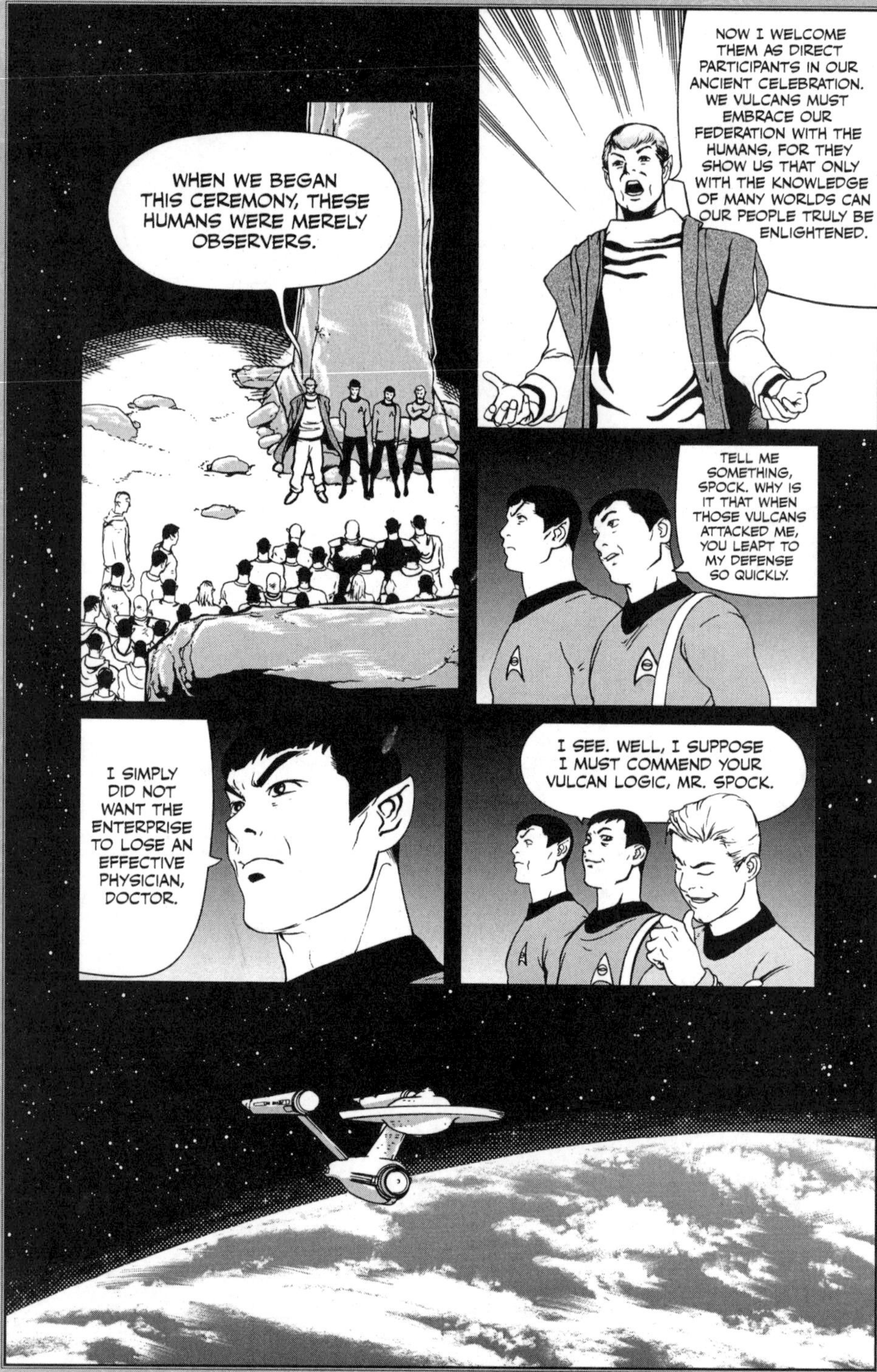
WHEN WE BEGAN THIS CEREMONY, THESE HUMANS WERE MERELY OBSERVERS.
NOW I WELCOME THEM AS DIRECT PARTICIPANTS IN OUR ANCIENT CELEBRATION. WE VULCANS MUST EMBRACE OUR FEDERATION WITH THE HUMANS, FOR THEY SHOW US THAT ONLY WITH THE KNOWLEDGE OF MANY WORLDS CAN OUR PEOPLE TRULY BE ENLIGHTENED.
TELL ME SOMETHING, SPOCK. WHY IS IT THAT WHEN THOSE VULCANS ATTACKED ME, YOU LEAPT TO MY DEFENSE SO QUICKLY.
I SIMPLY DID NOT WANT THE ENTERPRISE TO LOSE AN EFFECTIVE PHYSICIAN, DOCTOR.
I SEE. WELL, I SUPPOSE I MUST COMMEND YOUR VULCAN LOGIC, MR. SPOCK.

Sneak Preview of TOKYOPOP's Star Trek the manga: Kakan ni Shinkou